CRACKED OPEN:

Living The Dream

By J.C. Amberchele

NON-DUALITY PRESS

UNITED KINGDOM

CRACKED OPEN

First edition published July 2014 by Non-Duality Press

Non-Duality Press | PO Box 2228 | Salisbury | SP2 2GZ
United Kingdom

ISBN: 978-1-908664-40-2

www.non-dualitypress.org

It used to be
That when I would wake in the morning
I could with confidence say,
"What am 'I' going to Do?"

That was before the seed
Cracked open.

—Hafiz

TABLE OF CONTENTS

INTRODUCTION

This book is a collection of reflections and observations about life before and after I came to prison, as currently seen from the perspective of this Awake Emptiness at my core. I am profoundly grateful to the late Douglas Harding and his friends for helping me to see Who I Really Am, and to thus break the bonds of contraction and confusion that defined my criminal past. Truly without deserving it, I have been blessed with the miracle of inner freedom, the turnaround of turnarounds, what Harding referred to as the no-meter path to heaven.

This book is about living and failing to live the awakened life, and how discovering one's Emptiness—one's divinity—is the difference between the two, which, as it turns out, were never two to begin with.

As Harding often said, you cannot fix yourself from the level of the self. Only the One who is Other and yet not other, who is both No-thing and Everything, who is at the very heart of you as Who You Really Are, can transform your life.

ARRIVALS

I was in the delivery room when my daughter arrived. I later told friends that it was like being on LSD, except I didn't come down for days. I missed my son's arrival because it was by way of emergency caesarean, but when I saw him the next day I thought he was even more beautiful than his sister at that early age.

I can't count the number of friends who have unexpectedly arrived in my life. Looking back, it seems as though they magically appeared, and then, as the years went by, disappeared the same way, never to be heard from again. Several have remained in touch, though, one in particular who for no reason other than his selfless kindness continues to write and send money when he can, even though he barely makes his rent from month to month. Others, all busier with their lives than I could ever pretend to be with mine, never fail to drop a line asking how I am or what I need. How I enjoy the arrival of their letters, each one a lifeline to a world I rarely see!

In my former life before I came to prison I often traveled to faraway places, some exotic, some I hoped never to visit again. I was always on the go, it seemed. But now from this Emptiness, this Basic Space of Awareness that I am, I see that, out of all the trips I took, I never really went anywhere, that every one of those places arrived here. Not once did I board an airplane or climb into a car or even walk next door; in fact, I have never gone anywhere in my life. The truth is that when I see Who I Really Am, I see that I have always been here in this now-moment, that I have never moved and never *could* move (for there is nothing *to* move), that every "there" I ever thought I went to actually came here, that every city or country I ever visited actually visited me. This is not something I imagine or believe, it is something I see, right now in this boundless Awareness within which each scene appears and disappears, each one unique and each always arriving, one after another, always within this profound Emptiness that I am.

Speaking of arrivals, I can't remember when I arrived on the scene more than seven decades ago, most likely because I didn't. I've read that some people remember their past lives and even their birth into this one, but perhaps if they investigated Who They Really Are they would see they were never alive, which is to say that they never died nor were born again. I once jokingly wrote that, if time flies, this must be the airport. I was referring to prison, of course, but that was before I saw this immutable and timeless Emptiness that I am. The fact is, this really *is* the airport—THIS RIGHT HERE—the ground for every arrival in the universe, including the universe itself.

And certainly the greatest arrival we can all experience is the arrival of this Vision to end all visions, although it is a different sort of arrival in that what is seen has always been here; it has simply been overlooked. How I missed it for most of my life or how I thought I was something other than what it is, is a mystery to me. Certainly I never intended to think I was housed in this body or that I had a mind of my own, but so I thought, and for too long it was a detriment to all the others I thought were "other." Thank God for this arrival of all arrivals, this marvelous Absence-Presence that can also be called God, and for all those who pointed this out to me, who literally *pointed* to THIS RIGHT HERE.

And finally, on the subject of arrivals, when I'm writing I'm never sure what will show up in the way of the next paragraph or even the next sentence, which is at times all too obvious, but usually the words flow unmediated and unimpeded (un-minded!) from this Alert Void *as long as who I thought I was gets out of the way.*

What follows, then, is the result of this not always successful departure of my imagined "self," but with luck it will get out of the way long enough to allow the words to point the way back to where they came from.

DISAPPEARING

Last year I received a letter from my wife saying it was impossible to write to me. We've been married forty years, and I haven't seen her in thirty. Two decades ago was the last time I spoke to her on the phone, and she hung up on me. A divorced friend says I have the perfect marriage.

When I met her in the '60s she was 19, had long red hair, and wore a purple mini-skirt. She smoked dope and knew Hollywood celebrities. She cornered me on a back porch in a California beach town and flirted my brains into mush.

Later I ran into her in LA, and soon after, we hit the road together, up to San Francisco, then to New York, Toronto, Kansas City, and back to the west coast. We rented apartments, we hung out with her pot-smuggler friends, we knew the hip and hippie crowd wherever we went. She dropped acid and binged on liquor and sang Janis Joplin songs in the shower. She got higher than high and played cards or did the dishes, then got high again. She slept with friends and left me for others, but somehow, even though I was living with other women, we got back together again. Eventually we had a daughter, and a year later were married in The Little White Chapel in Las Vegas, and nothing whatsoever changed.

I can't say I ever loved her. I felt adrift without her, but I don't believe I ever loved anyone, back then. Caught up in the drama of ego-self, I was a mess, warring out-wardly against the world and inwardly within myself. How can you love someone when you think you're someone yourself? I—who I thought I was—this image of myself I had built and believed and defended at all costs—got in the way, filled every moment in every scene to the exclusion of others. Having no clue that others—indeed, that everything—was myself, I treated them as objects, pieces to be moved in this all-too-serious game of "me versus the world," "me getting something from life." I never loved anyone. I needed them, and so I used them.

And so it went. And so did she, eventually, back to Mexico where I had once fled to avoid the law. She's still there, to my knowledge, living a life I know nothing about. And we're still married. In her letter she said she was old now, and she told of illness and the many oper-ations she's endured. She said she was afraid. She sent a tiny picture of herself, a copy of a driver's license photo. In it, although weathered by the wind of time, I see the same face I saw when she was 19 and left me reeling on that back porch so long ago.

Except the color is off. The smile is weak, and her eyes seem lost in the pale of her cheeks, as if she is disap-pearing, retreating into a morning fog.

Or is it me? Am I the one who is disappearing, and have I found a love too huge for the two of us, for who we thought we were?

MORE OF THE SAME

The north end of this cellhouse is sunk into the earth a good ten feet, solid as a munitions bunker. I sit below ground, as it were, here in this cell at my metal desk, pen in hand, gazing out my barred window with its ledge a foot above the raked dirt. A chain-link fence topped with barbed wire stands some twenty feet out, and beyond it, part of the administration building to the west and a view of the recreation yard to the east, then the double perimeter fences clustered with razor wire. In the distance are two rocky hills, one alive with piñon and sage, the other bristling with antennae and atop which sits a massive water tank, black as night, a red beacon blinking a feeble warning to low-flying aircraft. This is my view, never changing, always new.

It is December, sunset, Dvorak on the radio, and a fly lands on the outside of my cell window, walks haltingly in a fly-sized circle, then disappears into a purple sky. Where did it come from, where is it going? I wonder. How could it survive in this cold?

And the answer trips me, invades what is left of me: From this grand expanse and for the briefest of moments, awareness sees itself from this selfsame angle, and who but itself could create this momentary tingling of recognition, a universe that banged into existence 15 billion years ago with all the intention of this improbable fly landing on this frozen window, looking at itself from the only point and the only moment it could, right here and now? And what could be next but more of the same?

FRIENDS

One of my Buddhist friends here is nearly always in trouble. The word is that he holds the record for the number of disciplinary reports in a three-year period. He gets into fights. He argues with officers. He claims he's afraid that others will take advantage of him. Lately, however, there's been a change. He seems to have mellowed. He told us at our last monthly meeting that he's experiencing a sort of global vulnerability, as if something inside of him is dissolving.

Another Buddhist friend is the most victim-prone person I've ever met. He routinely gets beat up. I've heard that he gets angry at certain people and blurts out obscenities, which comes back to him as a sock in the jaw. He's also stubborn about the *Dharma*, which tends to come back and sock him in the jaw, as well.

Thirty years ago before I came to prison I had at least 50 friends, none of whom have written to me since, and who can blame them?

Last month a friend in this cellhouse dropped dead of a heart attack. Another found out he has cancer, and a third just had surgery for a growth on his prostate. A friend here from India thinks Buddhism is the worst religion in the world because it makes you weak—look what it did for Tibet, how Tibetans simply gave in to the will of the Chinese without a fight!

My Indian friend is good friends with my surgery

friend but doesn't like my cancer friend, which makes it difficult for my surgery friend because he's friends with all three of us. This happens a lot here. There are little dramas within larger dramas within the Really Big Drama. Sometimes it's stressful but usually it's amusing. I'm grateful that no one has asked me to take sides in this latest little drama, because I couldn't do so. How could I believe in the little dramas when I can't even believe in the Really Big Drama?

Then there's my friend Melvin. Melvin is eighty-something, is overweight, has diabetes, and can't get his false teeth to fit right. He resembles a bulldog. To most, Melvin is, as they say, two cards short of a deck. He rarely talks, but when he does, he seems to know nothing about anything. He chuckles a lot, and usually when nothing is funny. Moreover, he seems oblivious of the past or future, as if he were lost in the present, although "lost" isn't the right word because he's quite in the thick of it. He simply has no complaints: no one has ever heard him complain about anything.

Melvin does what he's told. When he visits my cell, if I invite him to sit, he sits; otherwise he stands and looks at me. If I ask him a question, he answers, although not always with regard to the question. Last week a guard woke him up at three o'clock in the morning and demanded that he report to his job at the back gate, so Melvin got out of bed and got dressed and shuffled all the way to the back gate in the freezing cold, even though he didn't have a job there or anywhere else. When he arrived, another guard said they had made a mistake, and sent him back. As far as Melvin was concerned, it wasn't an inconvenience, it was just the way things were. Melvin isn't a Buddhist, but sometimes I think he's the Buddha.

These days I have new friends worldwide. I am amazed at their openness and kindness and generosity. At times when I grow small and am sure I'm a pig, I can't imagine why they would want anything to do with me. And then I'll get a letter from one or another of them saying whatever it is that true friends say, and suddenly it makes no sense that I think I'm my name and history, especially when *they* don't think I'm my name and history. But what marvelous sense it makes seeing and being Who I really am, which is Who we all really are: the One and the many! What marvelous friends we are, every one of us, in spite of ourselves!

A DAY AT THE BEACH

My daughter was two when I took her to New York to see a plastic surgeon. She had been bitten by a dog the year before, a nasty gash across the bridge of her nose and a three-inch rip in her cheek. He examined her scars and said he couldn't do anything until she was twelve.

We stayed at the Waldorf Astoria, me in my jeans and she in her tiny flowered muu muu and wooden clogs. We ate fabulously expensive Waldorf hamburgers, and in the morning we marched into F.A.O. Schwartz and bought an inflatable boat big enough for the two of us, bright yellow and decorated with cartoon seahorses and goofy fish, bow to stern. From a friend, I borrowed a Cadillac convertible, and we cruised like movie stars down the Garden State Parkway to the Jersey shore. It was summer, time to see my dad, and time for him to meet his granddaughter.

She loved the ocean. She sat like a frog in the middle of the boat and shrieked at the waves and cooed at the spray in her face. My dad sat under an umbrella on the beach and watched us, squinting. In the evening he drove us in his company car to his favorite restaurant— he wouldn't go near the Cadillac; I think he thought it was stolen, or that I had taken up with mobsters in the city and the car was a nefarious gift. We ate fresh-caught flounder, and my daughter fell asleep face-down in her ice cream, and then he drove us back to his apartment and bedded us down in the spare room, telling us how much my mother, then dead and gone three years, how much she would have enjoyed this day.

It was indeed a fine day, and as it turned out, the last day I would see him, and the last day my daughter would see him also. Some years later after my son was born and when I was doing a stint in a Mexican prison, my wife phoned him and asked for money, but he refused. He was a good man. He worked hard all his life and tried to be a good father, while I in turn adored him and blamed him, and in the end may have broken his heart. He died nearly a decade after that day at the beach, the same year, I was told, that I caught this case in the States and they locked me away for good.

Odd, how these stories, once ignored or forgotten, are now told with the shock of loss. Open, vulnerable, I find no way to avoid them. They arrive unbidden, painted with emotion, and leave only when they've had their say. I was his "Sport," his "Bub," names that said he loved me, and in one sense he'll always be my dad, but in another he is far more, as am I, then and forever, seeing that we all see from this selfsame Eye.

CHRISTMAS

Christmas Day, and a pall hangs over the prison. Men line up for the three working phones on the cellhouse wall. Outside, snow falls from a dreary sky. The chaplain makes his rounds, briefly stopping at each cell to shout "Merry Christmas" through the door. Years ago they passed out Salvation Army presents to each inmate—one plastic mug, one pair of socks, one pack of cigarettes—but these days it's only a greeting on the run. In the Control Center, a guard wearing a Santa hat watches the chaplain walk the tier.

Dinner is pressed turkey, yams, mixed veggies and mashed potatoes. We wait in a long line outside the chowhall in the snow for this special meal, one of only two each year when they serve cranberries. Inside, men advance along the wall single-file and eventually arrive at a window for a tray. Officers direct us to our row, and twenty minutes later, direct us to leave, making room for the hundreds of men yet to arrive. A friend remarks that we are blessed to eat such a meal that half the world's poor may never see, and when I neglect to answer, he looks at me with eyes too forlorn to be grateful, snowflakes melting on his prison cap.

||||

Philadelphia in the 1940's, Christmas Eve in my parents' two-bedroom duplex. Electric candles glow in the living room windows. The tree is lavishly decorated, and last year's toy train plies an oval track around the presents at its base. I am five or six years old, fresh from a nap, and my mother announces that Santa has already come and gone. I am nearly sick with excitement, and I tear into the presents—a soccer ball, an erector set, a wind-up jeep and several toy soldiers, a reindeer sweater and gloves—and then my dad calls me to the dining room and unveils the grandest gift of all: a Radio Flyer wagon with a big red bow on the handle. The next morning I choke down breakfast and run next door to see what my friend Frankie got, and when I finally tug him to my yard and show him my Radio Flyer, his jaw drops. But before we can try it on the sidewalk out front, I feel myself give way to what I should have done before breakfast. I've pooped my pants, and when I race inside and up the stairs to the bathroom, I'm worried I won't get to play on Christmas Day. My mother takes my soiled clothes and draws a bath. When my father comes up, he lectures me and sends me to my room, but later relents. The following week when I do it again, he takes his belt to me.

Years later in our new home in Germantown, my father refuses to buy me a BB gun for Christmas. Instead, he constructs a spectacular Lionel train set in an empty bedroom on the third floor, one that takes two weeks to build and only two days for me to lose interest in. I am ten years old, and although I am mostly interested in sports, I receive clothing from my aunts and uncles who are visiting. My grandmother on my father's side has dementia, and on this Christmas she forgets where she is and repeatedly tells my mother to answer the phone, even though it hasn't rung all day. I want to go to my friend's house where there is a real Christmas, but my father insists I stay and entertain my relatives. I feel trapped as if in a giant vise, and with each condescending pat on the head, it tightens yet another turn. I have long since abandoned the fantasy of Santa Claus, and several other fantasies, as well.

In high school I go to church with my girlfriend on Christmas Eve, then spend the night on her parent's couch and nearly all the next day with her family and friends. We get drunk on eggnog, and when I finally go home, my father reads the paper and my mother putters silently in the kitchen. I somehow feel I'm an accessory to an enormous lie, but don't know what it is. I love the neighborhood lights, the Christmas carols, the decorated stores, but something seems missing, and for that I experience an unrelenting sense of guilt.

Two years ago a new warden here decided to string Christmas lights on three small evergreens next to the administration building out front. They are lit again this year, coloring the snow on the prison lawn beyond the fence where we cannot go. Returning from the chowhall after our Christmas meal, a man behind me tells his friend that if he could get at them, he'd smash every bulb and tear the wires to shreds. To him and to many others here, the lights are an affront, the cruelest form of mockery—or as one man told me, "a goddamn Saint Nick smackdown!"

I stop to tie a shoe, and the men pass by, grumbling. When I stand again, I notice I am alone, and it is strangely peaceful. The air is crisp, alert. Snowflakes drift feather-like to the sidewalk. Beyond the fence, the trees glow like multicolored jewels in this nameless Void. Everything is as it is—shimmering, alive—a gift never to be repeated. Back at the cellhouse, I find my cellmate watching *It's a Wonderful Life* on TV. Snow clings precariously to the bars outside the window. A paper Christmas tree decorates our shelf, and a dozen cards sit wedged behind an electrical conduit along one wall. At the commercial break, a car salesman dressed as Santa Claus tells us to come on down, he'll make us a deal. Even this seems worthy of the moment, an invitation to the sacred, the open secret birthing in our heart of hearts.

PAROLE HEARING

There was a convict here nicknamed Gordy who was known throughout the prison for his hustle: You name it, he could get it for you, whether he had to buy, borrow, or steal it. I knew him because we were in group therapy together, which is to say that I knew his history and how he operated. In the end, he did a total of twenty years before he finally killed his number and got out.

One day in group it was revealed that the reason he'd never paroled early was because he'd smuggled a jar of Vaseline into the parole room and slammed it on the desk in front of the hearing officer, a State Parole Board member. He'd done this not once but two years in a row, and both times he was ejected, not to mention rejected.

I bring this up because I went to my first parole hearing this year, and I can't say I didn't think about Gordy and his jar of Vaseline, the wordless satisfaction he must have had at halting the humiliation before it began—Wham!—and then the trip to the "hole," hands cuffed behind his back, a chuckle under his breath.

Parole hearings are no fun, especially after an eight-hour wait on a metal bench in the anteroom. I remember as a kid going to the dentist, the anxiety during the days leading up to the appointment, the terror in the chair—and this first parole hearing was much the same, except this time it wasn't my mouth open under the light, it was the remnants of my neurotic and vulnerable self. Mentally I stumbled before the ordeal began. The hearing officer read from a laptop and spoke like a robot, and finally when he was done with the questions and my ill-prepared answers, he switched off the recorder and told me to leave.

The Board set me back five years. Five years until my next hearing, which in one sense was a relief, but in another....

... And here I was going to say "disappointment"— but truthfully, try as I might, I can't find a disappointed bone in my body.

But why? Considering I'm not entirely bald, why am I not tearing out my remaining hair? Am I so institutionalized that I no longer care about getting out? Now in my seventies—and as an aging friend used to say about himself from time to time—with my "shelf-life" getting short, shouldn't I be yearning for all the freedom I can get?

The problem with this sort of thinking is that it is based on an assumption that is fundamentally untrue. Pretending I am a regional appearance, a human being, a separate and self-existing body-mind giving rise to my own separate consciousness, I am living the lie of separation, known by some as the "original sin." Assuming this limited identity, I can never be free, no matter where I am or what I do. Even what I think is freedom will be seen to be temporary and relative, a passing scene in the play of life. The rest, if I'm lucky, will be a matter of distraction, anything to keep me from disappearing into the unknown.

Ironically, however, it is within that very unknown that freedom lies. Seeing beyond belief, seeing that the past and future lie in the now-moment of primordial awareness, I see my true identity—without question what I truly am—and yet I cannot say what that is, only that it is here and now and nowhere else, only that I am Presence itself. And having seen this, it is impossible to go back to the lie of separation; that is, it is impossible to place my identity there, to believe I am one of my appearances and not this empty and conscious capacity for all.

A friend visited this past weekend. While sharing the seeing of what we really are, she happened to mention something said by the contemporary sage Adyashanti which she had heard online: that the only difference between those who are awake and those who are not is in where they place their identity—either with awareness, or with the body. And what struck me was that, even though there is no middle ground, even though it is either one or the other, it is still only awareness that we are. Even when identified with the body, I am awareness pretending to be a body. Even in separation, I am the One who is all.

I do this. I step into the story, knowing all along it's a story, often reacting in accord with a lifetime of conditioning. Except that now it is impossible to be disappointed. Everything is more lightly held, more easily managed. More often than not I find relief, not only from past and present burdens, but relief simply for the sake of relief. And the idea that I could be freer in some other place or at some other time—well, that's simply nonsense.

But oh how the story beckons! And how marvelous it is to play all the parts!

FEAR

In a manner I can't quite explain, I think I was born terrified. My feeling is that, all of my young life—at least until I was seven or eight—I was afraid. Of what, I can't say, although it would manifest as panic from time to time in episodes that are some of my earliest memories. I couldn't stand being left alone, or alone with someone I didn't know. I remember scenes in my early childhood when babysitters had no choice but to call my parents because of the fit I was throwing. And there was the scene with a new nanny on a kiddie rollercoaster at an amusement park when I was paralyzed with fear, and another in a pool with a swimming instructor. These were years during which I couldn't have foreseen the possibilities of what might happen, such as total abandonment or a coaster car flying off the tracks or drowning in the pool. It was simply raw fear, immediate and unmediated, and oddly enough, it would disappear for all of my later childhood and my early adult years, but then return with a fury during the latter part of my LSD days, and later with the loss-of-control issues during my first glimpses of Emptiness.

(In those moments when I needed an explanation, I would sometimes wonder if I'd been born scared because I'd died scared, like I'd met some horrifying and violent end in a former life.)

Come to think of it, the fear *didn't* disappear during

my later childhood and early adult years. The panic was gone (or suppressed), but there was always an abiding sense of something wrong, something missing, some dread lurking just below the surface of my life. I was afraid that things were not as they seemed, that I was a pawn in a game I knew nothing about, that I was the fall-guy of a fabulous hoax, that at any time, unless I kept it propped up, the world would collapse around me in a hail of insanity.

But the fear did come to an end when I profoundly saw this awake Emptiness that I am, an Emptiness that is not only at the core of everything, but *is* everything. Indeed, and to put it mildly, things weren't as they seemed.

However, I find that an uncomfortable feeling—not dread; I can't call it dread—creeps back in from time to time, and when it does, I know that Emptiness has contracted into the game of self and other. And it is this feeling of discomfort that signals the turnaround, the metanoesis, that brings me back so that I am once again whole—or to be more specific: There is once again Wholeness, and no "me" or "I" to be apart from that.

How simple, how easy, and how well it works! Emptiness taps Itself on the shoulder and once again basks in the joy of its Self-seeing, Self-knowing, Self-being.

COMINGS AND GOINGS

For years there were ravens here, a family of ten or more. You'd see them perched like black-robed sentinels at the corners of the cellhouse roofs, cawing. They feasted on our garbage. They plucked worms from the lawn and stole the bread crumbs we threw out for the sparrows. By their mere presence they harassed the pigeons and squirrels. To my way of thinking, they ran the place. Even the cats were afraid of them.

One day they were nowhere to be seen. The rumor went that the staff, in an effort to reduce the population of pigeons roosting in the air-handlers, had strewn the roofs with poison corn. It was true—there were far fewer pigeons that following week, and the assumption was that the corn had killed off the ravens too.

Then came the rabbits. Soon the prison was over-run with them, far more than the great horned owls and snakes and cats could deal with. They were everywhere. In broad daylight they hopped onto handball courts and into the weight pile. They dug holes and hung out under the razor-wire between the perimeter fences. They foraged in the recreation yard and chased one another on the baseball diamond. They waited on the lawn outside the chowhall for an apple or a carrot or sat in the rain gutters and eyed us passing by on the sidewalk. Once, in the dirt outside my cell window, I watched a scruffy male with a torn ear slowly nod off to sleep, his hind legs splayed out behind him like a dog.

But suddenly the rabbits were gone, too. An officer told me that most were netted at night by staff on the graveyard shift, but this seemed unlikely—there were too many, and what about the hundreds under the razor-wire or in their holes? Still, day or night now, it is rare to see even one, and then only at a distance. Where did they go? What prompted them to leave?

What to make of these comings and goings in a place that is built to be sterile and lifeless? Spiders, as it turns out, are walking brains, and how better to experience the fruit of their thought than to gaze upon the intricacies of their webs? But in winter they are gone also, and if I'm lucky, an officer will let me out behind the cellhouse to clear the webs from my window, red with dirt and laden with the bodies of bugs sucked dry. Last fall I caught a spider in my bed. It crawled onto a sheet of paper I'd put down, and I carried it to the hallway outside my cell, but before I could place it in a safe corner by the wall, it jumped from the edge of the paper and bungeed all the way to the floor on its silk, a strand I couldn't even see. I marveled at its grace, feeling oafish and clumsy by comparison.

The cats were a joy. All were feral but one, an old tom who made his rounds looking for love, yawling. I never saw so much food smuggled from the chowhall, especially on chicken nights. The cats hid in the sewers by day and came out in the evening at chow call. Occasionally I'd hide a chunk of hamburger in my coat pocket, or the skin off a chicken leg wrapped in a napkin. Even though it was against the rules to take food from the chowhall, cats came before rules, and obviously the cats felt the same. And then, after nearly two years and several litters, they were nowhere to be found. A friend said they had made parole, and for all I knew, he was right.

And what will come next? A covey of pheasants? Improbable as it may sound, a dozen chuckers escaped their pen at a local ranch and found their way to the only other place safe from the marauding coyotes that roam the land outside the prison. At first, no one knew what they were. "They look like dinner," a man said to me, but how could anyone kill such a handsome bird, and anyway, how would you catch it?—they run as fast as they fly. And yet we watched their numbers dwindle day by day until, like the rest, they were gone. They were trapped and returned to their owner, we were told, but no one believed it.

Lately there have been few wildlife sightings. It is winter, and geese occasionally fly over, squawking in the frozen sky, but the yard is barren and the fields beyond the fences are brown and still. Another couple of months, and the weeds and flowers will be back, and along with this greening, the insects and migrating birds. And then, once again, prisoners and guards alike, we will be hard-pressed to ignore the mysterious pulse of God, these comings and goings that never end.

BLAMING

A Buddhist friend said to me, "Knowing that you can't do it wrong can be both frightening and freeing, because it takes away all sense of personal volition."

And I thought: frightening or freeing because one believes one is a separate self, "intrinsically existing" (as Buddhists would say), an entity that can act or not act on its own. Frightening because realizing that one can't do it wrong threatens that very belief in a separate self; and freeing because the dropping of that belief is the dropping of an intolerable burden, all the baggage of a life story willfully lived.

In reality, we, as who we think we are, are not responsible. We are not separate selves. A separate self is only one of an infinity of appearances, all linked together in an impossibly vast network of causes and conditions, and what we truly are, the only thing we can be said to be, is that totality, so that ultimately there is nothing to lose and nothing to be free of.

This prison has its share of obnoxious people, staff and inmates alike. Sometimes I catch myself blaming: it is so much easier to blame someone than to *be* them. Somewhere I read that when you talk badly about others you are only spreading rumors about yourself, and it is this that reminds me when the blaming starts, that stops me in my tracks and reveals that I *have* no tracks, that none of us do. Only the totality is responsible. Only the totality does anything, and does it both *within* itself and *as* itself. Only the totality functions at all, and does so with the intelligence and precision that itself can only marvel at.

Consequently, no one can do it wrong: no one as the separate self they think they are, and no one as the totality they really are. Which is another way of saying that no one has ever done anything, and nothing has ever been done.

So who's to blame?

RETROSPECTION

Years ago I went to India. It was during the war in East Pakistan, and millions of refugees had fled to Calcutta where they were living and dying on the sidewalks. Each night a truck stopped to pick up bodies in front of my hotel. There was no trash in the streets. My first day there, a naked man begged for my shoes. He said he wanted to eat them. I passed out rupees, but whenever I did, people mobbed me. I was afraid. I got sick. I went there with $50,000 to buy hashish, and left a week later with no money and no hash. On the flight back, a woman got drunk and tried to jump out of the plane. When I came home empty-handed, the friends who had fronted the money were incredulous.

Then I went to Spain. This time I took my own money. I also took a girlfriend and her mother because I was too neurotic to be alone. I rented a villa on a hill above the Mediterranean. In a nearby village I regularly got drunk on red wine that cost 18 cents a liter. The beach was rocky and the sea was polluted with human feces. I went there to score hashish in North Africa, but instead bought a car and drove like a maniac throughout Europe. My girlfriend wrecked the car. In Geneva she choked on a piece of meat in a fancy restaurant and coughed it up on the sleeve of a matronly old woman at the next table. We flew back to the States. I was broke. My girlfriend's mother was mad at me. I went back to my wife, but a few months later wished I hadn't.

All of the above is true, except that, from the point of view of this Infinite Emptiness, nothing ever happened. Each moment was seemingly experienced only in retrospect, and then even that was gone, just as these current memories fade in and out, and never are they anything other than an expression of this Infinite Emptiness.

Shocking, isn't it?

ANOTHER DAY IN PARADISE

Around here a favorite answer to the question "What's up?" is "Oh, you know, just another day in paradise."

I have a friend who never sees the majesty of the cloud formations in the morning sky, never notices the purple mist draping the mountains to the west, is never moved by a sunset or the moon on a winter night. We walk in the yard or to the chowhall together and he invariably recounts yet another version of his story, the same story we all tell every minute of every day: his successes, his problems, who said what to whom, what was on TV or what happened at work, what he would do if he got out. Sometimes it irks me, sometimes it breaks my heart. Above all he teaches me who I am not, and I love that he is myself, mirroring back this lesson of all lessons. And what a fine job he does!

I have another friend who was born five years after I came to prison. The energy of his youth sometimes startles me. Recently he discovered the awake emptiness at his core. Now when we meet he tells me how he sees he never goes anywhere, that the sidewalks and fences and buildings pass by and into the emptiness that he is, that what he is is utterly still. He talks of Yogananda and Ramana Maharshi and Muktananda, and sometimes his enthusiasm bubbles over into confusion. He laughs a lot, or suddenly grows quiet when he catches himself in a story. It's a joy to vanish in his favor, and I love that he is myself, mirroring back to me Who I Really Am.

Occasionally others wonder what I would do if I got out. Where would I live? How would I support myself? Who would hire an elderly ex-con with no work history or driver's license or even an address? I usually answer that I don't know, but really, this idea of being homeless and jobless is nothing if not amusing, although I know it is of the utmost importance to some, especially the Parole Board. "I am not in the world, the world is in me," I told a friend on the phone one day. My experience is of always being "at home," and my job is the moment by moment self-creation of the universe, exactly as it appears, including everything this body and these hands get up to. "I am the CEO of Myself," I added, "always at work, always at play, and let me tell you, the bonuses are great!" There was silence at the other end, and then my friend chuckled and offered me a place to stay, if I ever got out.

There are characters here, too, many with shaved heads and snap tempers, tattooed like circus freaks. If they call me anything they call me "Pops" or "Old School," but mostly they ignore me. The going thing these days is having facial tattoos. One man has the whites of his eyes tattooed black; another, the words "Love" and "Hate" on his eyelids. I told a man one day that I wanted a tattoo on my face of someone else's face, and he looked at me like I was nuts, or perhaps he thought I was mocking him. These men are serious, and seriously paranoid. Life to them is a dog-eat-dog struggle, and without the support of a gang, there is no question which dog they'll be. In such darkness, I see myself unraveling, dying each moment, lost in the frozen hell of my past. And even this is a beautiful thing when seen from this Clarity here and now.

There are three ex-attorneys here. There was a doctor here who shot his wife. There are college professors and military officers and even an ex-guard or two. A friend was a Benedictine monk; now he's doing life in a different sort of monastery. There are truck drivers and car salesmen and construction workers and drifters and plenty of career criminals, all doing time in their new job of prison inmate and never realizing their real job as God Himself, disguised as whatever imaginable. And to anyone who wakes up to this radical fact, I would say that their place of residence and their occupation is forever changed. They are, as we all are, the one living presence at the center of the universe, creating every marvelous minute of everything possible.

Just moments ago a man stopped outside the next cell and said to my neighbor, "Hey, what's happening?", and my neighbor said. "Oh, you know, just another day in paradise."

Little does he know!

A QUESTION OF CHOICE

For years there was this debate in the head I once thought I had over the question of free will versus determinism, and although I doubted I was free of conditioning and could choose as I pleased, I also doubted that all was set on a predetermined course and that I never had a say in anything done.

But when I discovered I was headless and saw that I had vanished, the question of choice or no choice vanished as well. It became obvious that choice appears only in the dream, the story, and furthermore, that although choice may appear, there is no such thing as a chooser. When I looked here and saw No-thing filled with everything, I saw no separation. I saw only Oneness, and in Oneness there can be no chooser or that which is chosen hecause neither exists apart from the other. Looking here confirms it—all is Pure Subjectivity, and in Pure Subjectivity no question of choice arises. Concerning free will versus determinism, the point, as they say, is moot.

But what does this mean for the dream, how does this impact the story I call my life?

In one sense, nothing really changes. The apparent ego continues to make apparent choices, and everything gets done or not done according to apparent plan.

In another sense, all is seen anew. Although the story continues, it continues with a sense of relief, a calm assurance that everything is as it should be. Life seems lighter; dilemmas no longer overwhelm, and gone is the burden of personal responsibility, replaced by the joy of genuine care. Love awakens. Laughter reigns, and more often than not, what once seemed direly important now seems simply relevant. Events arise, remain for their allotted span, then pass on, and there is the knowledge that something beautiful has happened and yet nothing has happened at all. Always there is this paradox, this mystery that spawns astonishment.

But there is also sadness, and grief may arrive unabated, for when there is No-thing here there is no thing to stand in its way. I cannot ignore what arises; I cannot choose one emotion or one situation over another. Although I may tell myself I am accepting of all, I cannot accept or reject that which I am. It simply is, exactly as it is, and as it is is What I Am.

There is a flip side to the Oneness coin, however. The other side of "no choice, no chooser" is that, out of this Awake Vacancy at my core pours every choice imaginable; out of this Solitary Emptiness appears all the volition in the world. Here in this no-place resides, as it were, the One Chooser, about Whom little more can be said other than What I Am is Who He Is, appearing as any and every possible thing chosen, moment by apparent moment, comprising the story of my life, the history of the universe.

Either way, then, without having to choose, or choosing all that appears, I win. And perhaps there is only one choice to be made by anyone: Choose THIS, and the question of choice or no choice is answered.

IT'S ALL CRAP!

My cellmate is often in a funk. He frowns a lot, and others regard him as unapproachable. He says he has angry thoughts, usually about how he'll tell someone off, even though that someone may not even exist. He fantasizes about arguments he always wins. He pictures himself getting into fights with those who have somehow humiliated him. He mopes a lot. His favorite comment is, "It's all crap!"

I told him one day that he resists being joyful because he's so comfortable being miserable. I told him this, knowing that the same pattern is alive in myself. I also told him that, despite appearances, it's all per-fect—which isn't to say that miserable can't or shouldn't become joyful.

Then, remarkably, I found myself in a funk, having angry thoughts about him! For two days I grumbled, and when I wasn't grumbling, I moped. Finally, at the end of the second day, I told him I was in a funk, and he said, quoting what apparently had become *my* favorite comment: "It's all perfect!"

"I'll have to remember that," I replied, "particularly when it's all crap."

He, of course, is my teacher. Never is it the case that I am his. More than a mirror, he is what I am, as is everything else, and I revel in the display, grateful beyond measure.

Last week at a Messianic Jewish service, he stood up in front of 70 of his peers and spoke about how selfish he is, not realizing that just by being present he was a gift to everyone there. He told of his suffering, how because it was all about him and not about God, he had alienated his family and walled off his friends. He vowed from then on to "walk the walk," to let God take over his life. He told me this when he got back from the service. He said he received a standing ovation, that several men came up to him later and said how they had related to his story, that he had made a difference. I was glad for him. I was glad for all of them, all who, despite themselves, already "walk the walk," whether or not they know it.

LONELINESS

For five months during the time that my wife and I were separated I lived in a large airy hotel room overlooking Sabalo Beach in Mazatlan, Mexico. Every morning I ate at the same outdoor cafe down the street, every afternoon I got drunk, and nearly every night I went to a bar, a disco, or a whorehouse—or all three. I was intensely lonely. Sometimes I dated American women I met on the beach, and sometimes I dated Mexican women who took me home to meet their families, but mostly I was alone. In fact, I was alone even when I wasn't alone.

I remember my father telling me when I was a teenager that the worst feeling in life was loneliness. He was a loner, and held himself aloof even around my mother and his few friends. I didn't share his sentiments, then. I had felt heartbreak when a girlfriend moved to another city, and there was plenty of anger and envy and the usual teenage angst, but I don't remember being lonely, even though I was an only child. Then again, maybe I was so lonely for so long that I grew numb to it early on, that I buried it by wanting so desperately to be like the naive image I'd held of my dad: the strong, silent type that was fashionable in those days, especially in Hollywood films.

So he surprised me when he admitted he was lonely. He told me he hated being alone, that he'd had several one-night stands with women he'd met during business trips, that his weekly "Friday night with the boys" wasn't always with the boys. And a decade later when my mother died at a relatively early age, he remarried that same year, and I remembered what he'd told me about loneliness—I didn't like his new wife, but I felt for my dad and knew why he'd married her.

By then I was experiencing loneliness myself and doing what I could to avoid it. This was during my post-LSD days when fear also began to set in: fear of losing control, fear of going crazy, fear of the Absolute Nothing I'd seen all too well. I surrounded myself with those I considered friends, and I remember thinking that my friends, most of whom were still taking LSD and smoking pot, never seemed to be afraid or lonely. I began to think there was something wrong with me, and eventually of course I realized that there really *was* something wrong, that loneliness, like the irrational fear I was experiencing, was a symptom of a false belief that had been handed down to me from generation to generation, as it is to all of us.

Recently it occurred to me that loneliness could he the eighth deadly sin, and when I couldn't remember all of the other seven, a friend whom I'd asked brought his dictionary, and there they were: anger, covetousness, envy, gluttony, lust, pride, and sloth. And below, there was this: "Said to be fatal to one's spiritual development" (American Heritage Dictionary, 4th Edition).

But of course! Loneliness, fear—and if you want to add sex, drugs, and rock and roll—they are all fatal to one's spiritual development. But they are also the path, the way in, the fast track home, deadly sins you can ride all the way to eternal life, for like "Danger: Road Closed" signs on the highway, they point the way back: always, always, they remind you that you are attached to a thought that isn't true. They tell you what you are not, and thus point to what you are.

Eventually my wife and kids arrived in Mazatlan after her boyfriend was killed in a plane crash. I was glad to see her. I didn't trust her and I knew she didn't trust me, but I needed her, as she in her grief needed me. We drove south to Cuernavaca, rented a house and put the kids in school and pretended to be content, waiting, as it were, for the next upheaval in our lives. It would be decades before I'd realize that the only cure for loneliness was to be what I'd always been: the Alone.

NO PLACE TO GO

Today an officer approached me and said, "Let me ask you a hypothetical question: If I got you past the front gate, gave you my car keys and asked you to drive downtown and pick me up a six-pack of Coke, would you come back?"

"Yes," I said.

He smiled wryly. "Are you that institutionalized," he said, "or is there just no place to go?"

For a moment, I couldn't answer. I wanted to say that there was no place to go because there is no place I'm not, but I knew this wasn't his truth. From his perspective, this prisoner with this number was institutionalized and had no place to go—he once joked that my parole plan was a pine box—and yet the idea that I could he stuck here and reliant on the machinery of prison for my comfort or survival seemed ludicrous at best.

I said, "No, there's no place to go." And then I added, "So yes, I'd come back, even if the tank were full and there was money in the glove compartment."

But then the phone rang, and both the officer and the moment were gone. That night I dreamed I was in prison, but woke up seeing that prison is in me.

ANOTHER VIEW

In her writings Byron Katie states that there are only three kinds of business: yours, other people's, and God's. When you're in other people's or God's business, you experience pain. And then she adds—and this is the heart of the matter—that ultimately, even *your* business isn't yours. It's nobody's. It's God's, if you will, seeing that God is nobody, and God is, as she would say, the last story we tell, after which there is only freedom.

In prison there is a seven-letter word that is worse than all the four-letter words, and that word is RESPECT. Respect is rarely given but often demanded. It is fear-based. At best, to respect someone in prison is to honor their ego, and the bigger the ego, the more respect that is due.

Disrespecting someone here is a sure-fire way to get into a fight. Disrespecting a gang can be lethal. And conversely, to pass the day demanding respect is to inflict on oneself, not to mention others, a considerable amount of pain.

The problem is, it is sometimes difficult to know what constitutes respect. New arrivals, called "fish," too often disrespect others without having the faintest idea they are doing so. It's the little things—looking in a cell window, staring at someone in the chowhall, talking too loudly near a telephone—discourtesies you wouldn't imagine a convict would care about, but when they are ignored they are magnified all out of proportion. It can be a hellish situation for someone who doesn't know about "doing your own number," which is the prison equivalent of minding one's own business. And to make matters worse, the convicts who demand the most respect are often the ones who least respect others, who are so far into someone else's business, not to mention God's, that they have made it their own.

Prison is raw. I don't remember anyone so openly demanding respect when I was free and on the streets. The same power games operated, to be sure, but they were coated with social niceties and often unrecognizable. Here, the food chain is in your face, the stronger demanding from the weaker, all the way down the ladder from the toughest and least inhibited to the most recent victim-prone milquetoast. We are, in this distinction, more like our brothers in the animal kingdom, and perhaps deserving of the term.

But there is another view, one that, from what I've read, Byron Katie and others share. It is that the criminal, unlike those who are mired in complacency, is one who has gone to great lengths in his quest for God; one who will do almost anything—even kill his own children—in his effort to break the bonds of contraction, of separation, of his own tortured ego. He lives on the edge, and in his ignorance, he lashes out at others, never realizing they are appearances of himself, of Who he really is.

And what would happen if he were to awaken, if he were to suddenly discover that all along he had been punching at the extremities of his own dream? I've witnessed a man drop his affiliation with white supremacists and open his heart to the "window" (as he calls it) of his own emptiness, of *the* Emptiness, in one fell swoop. I know a man who quit drinking and drugging and who has been sober nearly a decade. I've seen a fighter become a daily meditator, a chronic complainer become a bearer of smiles, an anarchist become a lover of "what is." Some of these men came here with serious crimes and may be here the rest of their lives, but because their Eye is open they now generate peace and understanding. Not always, but as a rule. And not, as far as I can tell, in a deliberate way, but as a result of touching their essence, of seeing Who they truly are, of relaxing into the One who is All.

Prison is indeed a factory of longing. Longing for a good meal, longing to see the stars at night, longing for the company of loved ones, longing to just once experience a moment of silence. And always, there is this longing for freedom, a freedom that deep down we know has nothing to do with these bars and fences that confine us.

In the meantime, we long and we demand respect even though we don't deserve it. We long and think other people's business is our business. We long year after year after year, until finally we break, and our longing turns inward. And then we discover that all along we ourselves are what we were longing for.

THANK GOD FOR KARMA

I should have learned early on about karma. When I was seven I picked up a toad and squeezed it over a playmate's head so that it peed in her hair. She ran home crying, and the very next day I fell on a broken bottle and cut my knee so severely that my dad had to rush me to a clinic for stitches.

When I was nine I learned how to play baseball, and even though I knew that my friend was standing close by, I took a practice swing and clobbered him with the bat. A week later I tumbled down a flight of stairs and knocked myself out. The doctor said I had a concussion.

And when I was twelve a neighbor boy and I went hunting feral cats with throwing knives. After a week of trying, I managed to hit one with the wrong end of the knife, but as far as I was concerned, the deed was done, I had got my cat. Then climbing over a fence in his back yard, without being aware of it my pant leg slipped over a picket, and when I jumped from the top of the fence, everything but my leg hit the ground. It was a twist break, from ankle to knee, and I spent the next eight weeks in a full cast scratching my tortured leg with a coat hanger and vowing never to hunt an animal again.

The list of examples goes on, and I need hardly say that I remained a poor student of the karmic lesson, considering I've been locked up for over half my adult life. But strangely, out of nowhere came the ultimate of all lessons, a lesson not in how to prevent bad karma or create good karma but in how not to generate *any* karma. How, as it were, to be altogether karma-less.

It arrived with the discovery of what I really am, the realization that I am not a human being, that a human being is only one of my manifestations, one of an infinite array of apparent objects that come and go in continuous flux. What I really am is this conscious void filled with all that coming and going, so that I am not an object but the awareness in which all apparent objects arise, including all thoughts, feelings, and perceptions. And when there is no longer a separate person, when one is no longer asleep and caught in the dream, there is no "one" to either create or receive karma.

And karma, like the notion of a separate self, depends on time, itself a notion. Karma cannot function in the eternal now, in the timeless realm of no-self, of God. God, being no-thing filled with everything, aware capacity and what He is capacity for, is pure subjectivity, absolutely no-thing and absolutely everything, one and the same. How could karma operate in the void of no-thing? And in the plenum of everything, what part could karmically affect another part, when there are no parts?

Karma is an appearance in the dream we call "life," and as such is dependent on the appearance of dream objects and dream events. In the dream, karma is cause and effect. It is tendency, probability, interdependency. It is evolution and fruition and balance. Karma is every story ever told, intricately woven into the grandest narrative of all—the history of the universe.

But in the ultimate view—the only true view because it is seen from the spaceless point of "here" and

the timeless moment of "now," i.e., pure subjectivity—karma doesn't exist. In the ultimate view, karma appears, but nothing ever happens; stories are told, but no one ever tells them; dreaming functions, but never is there a dreamer. In the ultimate view, there is only What Is, seen from What Is, and it is what we are. Here, there is no place for karma, no time for karma, no thing other than THIS RIGHT NOW.

Shouldn't we thank God for that?

SPACE

Buddhist meeting today, 1:30 to 4:00 P.M. We chanted, and our teacher led us through a period of *Vipassana* meditation, directing us to focus on our heart center, then later to attend to the space in the room, to *be* that space. And all the while, here in this heart, in this space— thoughts and more thoughts, one after another: thoughts about the previous thought, thoughts about watching thoughts, a litany of thoughts gone before they can be captured and observed. In this way, each tiny fragment of the present seems to vanish in the noticing, and is thus noticed only in hindsight as yet another thought. Even space seems the most fleeting of memories, as if God Him-self—this great abyss of witnessing awareness—creates the world moment by moment only to apprehend it when the moment has passed.

At the end of our meditation session a discussion begins about the heart center, what we felt, what we thought. Some report feelings of warmth accompanied by notions of compassion and love—but here, not a sin-gle thought moves in that direction; I don't even know where my "heart center" is.

No one mentions space. No one seems to want to go there, so I blurt out the analogy of the house and how the space inside is the same space that was there before the house was built, how the walls and roof and floor are also made of space, how when the house is torn down, the same space will still be there—and yet we called it a "house." And when I say that the house is like the body, and mention what remains when the body dies, no one says a word, and suddenly I realize I've said too many, said what maybe never needed to be said to begin with.

The silence is pregnant with a sort of fidgety anticipation; we sit leaning forward on our chairs like lemmings peering over the edge of a cliff.

Finally, the teacher announces that it's time to stretch, a little yoga, and I shed the chair and step into space, feel myself give with the first pose, expand to the limit with the second.

EX-CONS

Today I called my friend Kelly who is an ex-drunk and an ex-drug addict. He "woke up" right here in prison several years ago, got out, and has been clean and waking up ever since. I asked how things are going for him, and he said it's like blowing up balloons—every day several times a day you blow up this balloon of non-sense, and then suddenly you look back at this infinite no-thing that you are and the balloon pops and all the air rushes out of every balloon you and everyone else ever inflated, and then, after the sigh, after the smile and the laughter, the next balloon appears, and in goes the hot air. This is how it works, he said. This is the game. This is the holy matrimony between self and other that is never other than Self.

I swear, talking to Kelly is like talking to God.

Then I called my friend Derek. Derek is a paralegal who after nearly two decades got himself out of prison twice on the same case. Now he's doing well: He has a job, an apartment, a car, and is part of a veterans program for those with post-traumatic-stress-syndrome. He laughs a lot. His favorite expression is, "Film at eleven," which he tacks on at the end of every letter I get from him explaining what he's doing or hoping to do. In prison Derek used to be my jogging partner, but now that he's out and is older he's had health problems. His mother and brother recently died, and his son lives in California. Derek lives alone, but I've never heard him say he's lonely or sad. As far as I know, he has no assets, no savings account, no retirement plan. It's simply "Film at eleven."

I swear, talking to Derek is like talking to God.

Then I called Jerry. Jerry was here in the '90s but now lives back East. We've been in touch the last twenty years. Every three months he buys a $50.00 canteen "care package" for me, despite the fact that he struggles to make ends meet driving a truck for low wages. Jerry was a Marine. He graduated from college. It's not easy for an ex-con to find a good job. Now in his fifties, his strength isn't what it used to be. He lost his first job because of a hernia, and now in his new job he works nearly twice the hours for the same pay. He lives alone. On his day off, he spends most of his time helping others. He knows I like cheesecake but can't get it here, so occasionally he orders it for himself and dedicates it to me. He is loyal to the point of disappearing. He says I have a home if I ever get out—his home. Jerry is an ex-weightlifter who resembles Kojak but who writes poetry that can make you cry. He agrees that our longtime friendship is a first-class example of brotherly love, unconditional to the core.

I swear, talking to Jerry is like talking to God.

Then I called Curt. When he was here, Curt was the smartest guy in prison. He was also a student of "A Course In Miracles," a member of our Buddhist group, and a damn good musician. After ten years in, when he hit the streets he went to stay at a friend's house in a gated community but the neighbors found out he'd been in prison and made him leave. Curt is a computer expert, but for over a year he mowed lawns and shoveled snow and holed up in a rooming house just to survive. When his break came, it came big—now he works at a tech firm and makes more money than he ever did before he came to prison. He sends me jokes he's found online. He writes two-sentence letters because he's so busy. He and his new girlfriend host spiritual gatherings at their suburban home and are considering starting a zip-line business in the mountains. The last he wrote, he said he would soon have more time for himself, but I doubt that because there's not much of "himself" to have time for. Our phone conversations are always short. Usually I call him because I need something, and despite his busy life, he never fails to help.

I swear, talking to Curt is like talking to God. In fact, the truth of the matter is, talking to *anyone* is like talking to God. And delete the "like."

DAY TRIP

Today I went on a "day trip" to see an eye doctor downtown. These day trips out of the facility are a chance to glimpse a slice of the outside world without having to forfeit one's cell and job, both of which are lost during a longer stay at a hospital or clinic. The uncomfortable part is the strip search at the back gate and the ankle and hand restraints which are worn all day, wrists stacked one above the other and held in place by a black metal box, then chained to one's waist.

The van, fortunately, was new, the cage inside recently painted, the vinyl seats spotless. I've been transported twice before in the "dog van," a panel truck with a steel box welded inside, airless and hot, and into which they cram six convicts shoulder to shoulder on two metal benches. After my surgery for a hip replacement, they slid me in backwards on the floor because I couldn't climb into the box and sit on the bench. All the way back to the facility I prayed they wouldn't hit a pothole.

Over the years, I've seen the town grow almost to the outskirts of the prison. The ride to the eye clinic is a quickly passing show of prefab buildings and look-alike cars, strip malls and gas stations and fast-food joints slapped down one after another. At the clinic, another prefab, the officers hustled me in through a rear door and into an exam room, my chains rattling on the tile floor, and in a moment a smiling clinician in a pink smock entered with a laptop and asked a dozen questions to which I answered "no." Then came the dilating eyedrops, and twenty minutes later, the exam, one of the stranger and more amusing experiences of the day, several versions of what seemed like the same many-limbed apparatus slid in front of me and with the optometrist adjusting and peering, peering and adjusting—but peering into what? "Look to your left, look to your right," he said, all the while staring into this vast Nothing, shining his points of light into this empty room inhabited by no one.

Later, in another room, he said, "You show an increased level of intraocular pressure, a sign of glaucoma, so we're prescribing drops which you'll use daily"—and then he was gone before I could ask him a single question, and the officers escorted me back out the rear door and into the van—except now, perhaps triggered by all that peering, the opposite was happening: I didn't walk out the rear door and climb into the van, the rear door approached and passed around me into nothing, as did the van door and seat, with glimpses of upside-down shackled ankles and cuffed hands, and then amazingly the front half of the van with two officers on board accommodated a continuously changing and colorful array of city streets and speeding highway until the prison arrived and passed within me.

A friend approached when he saw me enter the cellhouse. "How'd it go?" he asked.

"It came and went well," I said.

"And did they find anything wrong with your eyes?"

"What eyes?" I said, and he looked at me like I'd gone mad, and in that instant I found myself back in a body and inside a building, imagining a face here, imagining it smiling.

STILL AND TIMELESS

The experience of being perfectly still came early on. It was seen. Awareness—What I Really Am—never moves, has never moved, while the scene moves through it. Walking, immutable Awareness sees the body striding, sees the pavement, fences, and buildings passing by, and sees the awake and luminous emptiness of Itself always "here." Even with eyes closed there is only aware stillness, through which all sensations come and go.

The experience of being timeless, however, came, as it were, later on. Being forever still seemed a matter of fact, while the experience of always "now" was elusive. But why, when they are so closely related as to be one and the same?

There is no answer. One experience simply arrived after the other, even though it was quite clear in the revelation that there was no "before " and "after," nor even a "one" or an "other." The actual experience of "now," of timelessness, is of Awareness aware of Itself and simultaneously aware of each moment arriving and departing through it. Moment in, moment out—Awareness aware of each arrival and departure but never in Itself aging or evolving, never being other than now.

What I Am (and anyone can say it) is Here, has always been right Here, and What I Am is Now, has always been right Now, including not only immutable and timeless Awareness but the scene appearing here and now as well. It is all simply Awareness, and this is What I Am, though I cannot say what Awareness is or where it comes from. I can say only that it astounds and confounds Itself, amuses Itself. And it is always enough.

SPARROWS FROM ROME

Twenty years ago there were two prisons where there is now one. To save money, they combined them, and to do so, they opened a gate between the two fences so that we now pass from one side to the other depending on what housing, work, or program areas we are assigned to. The gate is called "midway," and it is the year-round feeding ground for a good-sized flock of sparrows, probably 60 or more.

After the merger, they built a new chowhall on the west side, so that all of the east side inmates must pass through midway to eat, three times going and three times back. Although it is against the rules to take anything from the chowhall (except a piece of fresh fruit), nearly everyone does, especially if the item would taste better with a Ramen soup or rice or any of the other foodstuffs we can buy weekly from the canteen. The other reason to take food from the chowhall is to feed the sparrows, and the sparrows know exactly when and where that takes place: six, noon, and five-thirty, seven days a week, at midway.

Their favorite is French toast, followed by cornbread, then hamburger buns. They perch on the razor wire above the gate preening and calling and squabbling, but when the first slice of French toast hits the dirt below, they are on it in silence, tearing it from each other into smaller and smaller pieces in a frenzy of beaks and feathers. On a good day, ten slices will feed the lot of them, and nearly every day is a good day provided there is bread on the menu.

Once, during a winter cold snap as I passed by on my way to breakfast, I noticed a dozen or so sparrows sitting on the ground, their feathers puffed into balls for warmth. In front of them was a pile of spaghetti from the meal the night before. They seemed curious about it, but not curious enough to eat it.

My first thought was, What idiot would feed spaghetti to a bird? And my second thought was, How did he get it here? In his pocket?

And then just as I was leaving, a sparrow hopped forward and pecked at one of the frozen strands. Then another sparrow came forward, and another, and I thought, Well, who's the idiot now?

And who can question nature's way, which happens to be *every* way, just as it is? If I think birds won't eat spaghetti, and no one in their right mind would feed it to them, then I'm not in my right mind, which "right mind" happens to be *no mind at all*, just pure awareness for whatever shows up.

And as I walked away—backwards, watching the scene on the ground at midway—more birds arrived, and I had to admit, it was "Italian" for breakfast, and for all I knew, these sparrows had come all the way from Rome, just for this, just for this.

So why not? Every story counts, and maybe we're all idiots, pretending to be geniuses. Or vice versa.

HISTORY

My girlfriend and I flew to Amsterdam. It was the week before a major Woodstock-style concert, and thousands upon thousands of hippies were camped in the parks and on the sidewalks. In the States, this would have prompted a public outcry, or at the very least a police response, but what did the authorities in Holland do?— they went on television asking the citizens of Amsterdam to open their houses and take in a hippie or two until the concert was over. Problem solved.

Then we went to Copenhagen. My girlfriend had long black hair and black eyes and wore a diamond in her nose. Walking in the city at night, a man in a doorway asked us if we wanted to see a live sex show. My girlfriend said yes but I said no. Then he asked us if we wanted to perform in a live sex show. We walked on.

We flew to Germany. In Baden-Baden my girlfriend wanted to go to the baths, but all she had with her was her string bikini and everyone else was old. Instead, we went to a chocolate shop and I got sick eating too many chocolate truffles.

We drove down to Geneva for Swiss Independence Day. There were thousands of revelers on the quay with foam mallets, bonking each other on the head. Walking with my girlfriend, she got all the bonks, mostly from young men and mostly on her chest. The next morning we went to a parade contest in which a high school band from the United States took second place. I couldn't say why, and at the time it seemed almost embarrassing, but when the flag bearer with Old Glory marched by, my eyes filled with tears.

Back in the States, on a drive from Miami to Denver, we stopped at Disney World with a trunkful of cocaine. Two days later a thief stole her suitcase filled with cash from our motel room in Kansas City. She called the cops, then lied about how much money was in the suitcase. I prayed they wouldn't get suspicious and search the car. That night, we went to a club. The New York Yankees were in town to play the Royals. On her way to the ladies room, a famous Yankee infielder hit on her. She told him to get lost. Then later he came to our table and hit on her again, right in front of me. We got up and left.

We rented a house on the outskirts of Denver. One night, four hooded men woke us up at gun-point in our bedroom. They tied our hands and feet and ransacked the house. They wanted cocaine. My girlfriend was defiant, but I wanted them out of the house before they shot us, so I told them about a hidden compartment in the garage. They fixed themselves sandwiches in our kitchen. When they left, they stole my girlfriend's car but told us where they'd park it with the keys in the ashtray. This time she didn't call the cops.

We went to Mexico. I remained onshore while she went deep sea fishing. She caught a marlin, then spent five hundred dollars having it "stuffed" and shipped to her mother in the States. In Honduras we stayed at the same hotel in Tegucigalpa where the Miss Universe contestants were staying, and twice in the lobby she was asked which country she was representing. At the pool, there were so many CIA types with dark glasses that we got paranoid and drove to San Pedro Sula near the coast. On the flight from there to the States, we sat next to a family from Roatán who said they were descendants of pirates.

A week after I was arrested and thrown in jail, my wife happened to show up for a visit at the same time my girlfriend did. Neither one of them ever visited again. Years later my girlfriend's mother wrote to tell me that her beloved daughter had died of a seizure, and that I'd been her only love. She was only forty-nine.

CALLING THE SHOTS

Around here each gang has a "shotcaller," a sort of regional mob boss who plans the moves and decides which gang member should do what and to whom. As a joke, I tell people that I'm in the "Over-The-Hill" gang, and that Melvin, my tottering eighty-something friend, is my shotcaller—and not, by the way, someone you'd ever want to mess with!

A common racket and gang specialty in practically every prison is a form of strong-arm extortion known as "rent collection," whereby weaker (or solitary) inmates are forced to pay for their safety by purchasing canteen items for a member or members of the gang. So one day on a dare Melvin and I approached the two toughest guys on the tier, both of them tattooed weightlifters twice our size and a third our age, and told them we were OTH (Over-The-Hill) OGs (old gangsters), flashed our gang sign (hands twisted into arthritic claws), and demanded "rent" for the coming canteen period.

They glared at us for a full five seconds, a breath-holding eternity for me, and then they crumbled into loud guffaws and gave us each a manly fist-bump. And I thought: Sometimes this is how you get by, in prison, and sometimes you gain an ally you never thought possible. A week later I heard one of them say to a guy on the tier, "Anyone messes with those old men, messes with me."

Not that Melvin and I had it planned that way. The truth is, some years back, Melvin forgot how to call even his own shots, and these days it's perfectly clear that I've never called any myself, at least not as who I thought I was. Only the one Shotcaller Itself calls the shots, and in that moment-to-moment astonishing act calls into appearance Its very own Self, a divine racket if ever there was one, and one in which we all participate all the time, whether or not we know it.

And how relaxing it is to know that I've never done and never have to worry about doing anything, and at the same time that everything done is so effortlessly done by Who I Really Am! And of course the joke is that who I occasionally think I am is being done by Who I Really Am, and Who I Really Am is everything done everywhere, which happens to be here.

Incidentally, Melvin has reached the age or the stage where "Just Don't Know" has become the source of his happiness, and mine as well, which is why I call him my shotcaller. He's old enough to know less, and I'm getting there myself, and although we may be OTH OGs in appearance, by God we are eternal Love at our core, and who can mess with that?

ANOTHER VISIT

Oh, what have we here?—a squirrel on the ledge outside my cell window! A big male, regal in his robe of fur, flicking his tail and regarding me with his jewel black eyes.

"Where did *you* come from?" I hear myself say, and immediately he bounds from the ledge and zips out of sight.

But a moment later he is back, nose twitching at the glass, and I reach for my locker box and rummage in a canteen sack for what the moment demands.

Halfway up the window casing there is a hole in the corner of one of the panes, just big enough to fit the tip of my thumb and forefinger and a peanut through. When I do, he scrabbles up the side of the frame, places a tiny hand on my thumb, and gently takes the peanut in his teeth. My thumb tingles, my heart bursts, and tears well up from the depths.

His Majesty has spoken.

BOUNDLESS AWARENESS

Take the five senses. Draw a dot in the middle of the page and let that dot represent "I." Then draw a circle around the dot at a radial distance of, say, one inch, and let everything inside that circle represent the experience of touch and taste.

Now draw another circle a little farther out and let everything inside that circle represent the experience of smell.

And about a third of the way to the edge of the page, draw another circle and let everything inside it represent the experience of hearing.

Then all the way close to the edge of the paper draw one final circle, and let everything inside that circle represent the experience of sight.

And the question is: Why assume that the boundary between what is "you" and what is "not you" is located at the edge of the first circle?

Add thinking to the above, and what you experience is infinite, and yet it is that same thinking process that limits you to that which you consider to be "you," i.e., to the body located within the realm of touch and taste; while all else—no matter what it is or how close or far away it appears, and even though it too is sensed or experienced right here where everything else is experienced—you consider to be "not you."

For instance, seeing exactly what is presented and

not relying on what you believe or imagine, when you look down, the headless body you see is only a fraction of the total visual scene, and yet you consider only the body to be "you." Of the five senses, how is it that you draw the line at touch and taste, especially when hearing and seeing are the more prominent senses?

Looking up and out, the body can't be seen, and yet you are certain that nothing in the scene, except perhaps that nearby shadow or blur you assume is a nose, is "you." Relying only on what is currently presented and not on what you have learned, isn't it obvious that the scene, including everything you sense or experience right here, is your true body? In other words, isn't it obvious that your embodiment includes everything that awareness experiences, all at once, moment by moment?

Perhaps the question is not, "How could that be possible?," but "How could it be otherwise?"

SCHOOL

I was eight years old when I started to commute. I left home at dawn in North Philadelphia and took two trolleys to Germantown, then hiked a mile to school. There was a Nedicks on the corner where I got off the trolley in Germantown, and every day I would spend part of my allowance on a glass of juice and a sugar doughnut.

At school we all wore the same sweaters. There were no girls. My third-grade teacher was old and strict. Once, during class when I was digging in my pocket for a marble, she shouted, "We'll have none of that in here!" A couple of kids snickered, but most seemed as puzzled as I was. None of what? When I raised my hand and asked her what she meant, she said, "There'll be no playing with yourself in my classroom, young man, and if you do it again, you're going to the principal's office." After class, one of the kids told me his older brother did it, that it had something to do with sex but you got pimples from it.

Then my parents bought a house two blocks from my school. It had three stories, four bedrooms, and two dens. There was an enclosed porch, a yard with a hedge around it, rhododendrons and honeysuckle under the living room windows. Our furniture from the old house looked silly in this new one, but when my dad came home with a television set—as it turned out, the first in the neighborhood—I forgot about the furniture, even though most of the time there was only a test pattern on the TV screen. After that, the only time we listened to the radio was during the day or during summer vacations at the Jersey shore where the TV signal didn't reach.

A year later I discovered my dad's Esquire collection in the attic, and shortly thereafter, what my third-grade teacher meant by "that" when she said "We'll have none of that." By then I was a whiz at baseball. From third-grade on, our school teams played other schools in our conference. We had our own fields and umpires and uniforms and gloves and cleats just like the big kids, and we played our hearts out in front of small weekday crowds made up of mostly mothers.

Once, during the ride to an "away" game, with the entire team and the coach packed into four cars (driven by mothers), the kid next to me fell out the passenger-side door as we were rounding a curve on a busy expressway. He surely would have died had I not grabbed his shirt at the last second and held on while the car lurched to a stop. Later, they called me a hero, but I was no hero—I had been poking him, bullying him, and in his effort to get away from me, he'd moved as far as he possibly could against the door and, fending off another poke, his arm came down on the door handle and out he went. He never told anyone, and neither did I.

The last two things I remember about those early days at school were: 1) the day I hit two home runs in one game, then got beat up in the dugout by a peewee-sized kid I'd smarted off to; and 2) just before the last game of the season, while doing warm-up exercises in the grass, I had my first orgasm, and with it, the creepy feeling of having been caught with my hand in my pocket, fondling a marble.

High school was a blur of sports, girls, cotillions, and courses barely passed. Considering how little I studied, I was lucky to have scored the C's I did. My buddies and I wore buttoned-down shirts and chino pants and white buck shoes. We rode our Raleigh bikes to school and never locked them in the bike rack. We were "preppies," we were athletes, we were clean-cut to a fault... and sometimes after school we stole cars from the train commuters' parking lot and went for joy rides around the city. Thank God I graduated from high school, although I often ask myself why I never graduated from crime.

College in Pennsylvania was more of the same, only this time it was football and frat house beer. My grades were fair, except when I cheated, and then they were good. But at the end of my sophmore year I fell into a crisis and transferred to a school in New York City. There, I made the dean's list, and met the most beautiful woman in the world. We studied together. We joined the French club. We sang folk songs and hung out in Greenwich Village and slept together on an army cot in my otherwise bare studio on the Lower East Side. When Kennedy was shot, we wandered aimlessly through the city streets until we boarded a bus for Philadelphia, killed the night in a cheap hotel, and rode the first bus back in the morning. Why, we didn't know. She got pregnant, we talked of marriage, her father said I'd have to convert to Judaism. But then she found an abortionist on the top floor of a sleazy hotel on the West Side, and later when I graduated in June, I went to Hawaii and she went to the Sorbonne, and I never saw her again. Sometimes I wonder how it would have turned out, had we never parted.

Strange, isn't it, that here in this Emptiness with no name, no narrative, I can so easily sculpt a history by

69

means of a few fleeting and seemingly personal memories, each tucked away in some dusty corner of a "mind" I can no longer claim. And yet without them, where is there life? Where is all that we recognize as human? Who would we be for each other?

A FRIEND DIES

Clusters of perimeter lights sit atop one-hundred-foot poles all around this facility, each radiating an island of light, and each island merging with the next, so that nowhere is it dark. The stars never shine here. It's been 30 years since I've seen a star, but on winter evenings when we march to the chowhall, the moon can be seen, and Venus, and Jupiter when conditions are favorable, and sometimes the faintest glimmer of Mars above the prison glare.

A friend died yesterday. For three days he complained of chest pain, but at the clinic they said his EKG was normal. On the fourth day, he died. He was a Vietnam vet, a cook in the army and a cook after the war, and then one day while he was at work his wife and two young sons were killed in a car accident, and just like that, everything changed. Eventually he wandered out west and got into trouble, did twenty-two years in this prison and had only a year to go.

And that's how it goes, for some. Once, on the way to the chowhall when I pointed out Venus, he told me it wasn't Venus, it was the space station. I thought he was joking, but he grew angry when I laughed. And then I saw that, at that very moment, it *was* the space station. It was my friend and it was the space station and there was nothing here to oppose either, not a shred of matter, not a wisp of belief to get in the way. Just this silent

Emptiness, and my friend, and if he had called that crystal spark of light above us a celestial being of the highest order, an angel most divine, it would have been that, too, just as it appeared.

But now he is gone, and Venus hangs in the sky, and deep down I don't know what it is, or what THIS is, or what anything is.

FLOWERS

When you move your arm, what really happens? Countless wavicles at the quantum level collapse into one coordinated function that is passed "upwards" to trillions upon trillions of atoms at the next level which in turn activate trillions more molecules at a higher level which instantly signal billions of cells to contract a particular set of muscles, and "you" lift "your" arm. And all of this happens in a fraction of a second.

But where does the process begin? What is the impetus for this seemingly simple but impossibly complicated task? If it begins in the realm of countless particles (or the vibrating strings of which they may be composed), what prompts them?

Most would say that the impetus begins with a thought, that cells in the brain are activated by, say, a decision, and the message is then passed electrochemically via nerve fibers to the arm. But in the last decade or so science has demonstrated that the impetus to move one's arm actually *precedes* the thought, the decision, to move it.

I find this process utterly amazing, worthy of the highest reverence. I watch athletes perform on television, or a pair of swallows bank and dive outside my window, and I practically swoon with admiration. How *is* that done? And what I used to take for granted I no longer can: a man on the tier talking to another, the lips and tongue moving in perfect sync, the sound of his voice and the meaning conveyed—it all just boggles the mind.

Douglas Harding makes the point that the impetus is within the All, that there is a sort of two-way traffic of intelligence informing all the levels, from the no-point of Empty Awareness up through the subatomic and atomic and molecular and cellular and human and planetary and solar to the galactic and beyond; and vice versa, from beyond the galactic down through the subatomic, and that the impetus or "message" is non-local, i.e., is instantaneous, or simultaneous; is, in effect, timeless.

Thus a plant may appear to grow slowly, but the impetus for each now-moment is instantaneous, all the way up and down the levels, so that the plant, in each apparent nanosecond of its manifestation, is both a consequence and a representation of the All. Truly the plant is a bloom of the universe, as is everything else, animate or inanimate, natural or man-made. *You* are the universe blooming, a walking, talking flower of infinity.

When my son was five, my wife drove my daughter and him from Guadalajara to spend a week with me in Puerto Vallarta. By then he spoke fluent Spanish, and when we went to El Set, a touristy restaurant on a cliff overlooking the Pacific, he quite naturally addressed the waiter in Spanish and ordered for himself: *camarones al mojo de ajo*, with *flan* for desert. I smiled, my wife and daughter smiled, and the waiter quickly summoned the maitre d' who, after several bows, picked up my son and marched off with him to the kitchen where my son spent the next half hour "helping" prepare our meals. Talk about a flower of the universe! How he charmed them, this tiny *Norteamericano* surrounded by cooks, calling the shots in Spanish!

And oh how I wish I had seen then what I see now! How precious he was, and how perfectly unique! Over the next three years I would visit only briefly—by then I was living with another woman—and then when he was eight I caught this case and landed in jail. It was strange when he showed up a decade later at the prison to visit me, nearly a head taller than me and in his high school football jacket. I was so proud of him, and yet I hardly knew him, knew him as little as I knew myself.

It is only today that I see how exquisite he was, how exquisite we all are. Everything he did was a manifestation of this Love we call the universe: every smile, every cry, every time he picked up a toy or a bug and put it in his mouth, every time he charmed an adult or later studied at school or caught a football in the end zone, and even, near the end, even when he shot dope into his arm and fell to AIDS. Caught up in my stories, I never saw the importance of his, even the ones that led to his death at an early age. He blossomed all-out, no holds barred, and when his time came he died with love in his heart. Aren't we each like this in our own inimitable way, flowers of the All, and isn't our every moment, no matter how gross or subtle, the manifestation of this Love, this No-thing/Everything that we really are?

Just now an officer came to my cell. Standing in the doorway in his blue uniform, he is Krishna come to remind me that I have left a mop out in the hallway. I thank him, and he disappears as magically as he appeared, and suddenly what is left of me vanishes in favor of the passing tier, the tables and walls of the dayroom, the approaching hall—and there is the mop, leaning against the Coke machine. A hand reaches out for it, and a rush of emotion invades this Vacancy. "My God," I hear myself say. "How is that done?!"

EXCUSES

Here is something you don't often hear prisoners say: We make no mortgage payments, no car payments, no insurance payments, pay no rent, no utilities, no taxes, no food or laundry bills, no medical costs, no court costs, no transportation or fuel costs, no mental health or drug treatment costs, get free education, free vocational and on-the-job training, free pre-release support services, and free cable.

I'm not sure what crime victims get for nothing, but I'll bet the list is a lot shorter than the above. And here's the sad thing: For what I've just written, I could get beat up, because around here it's mostly about how *we* are the victims—victims of the law, of the police, of the courts, of the Department of Corrections, of the prison facility, of the guards. Very few fully accept the fact that their past actions have brought grief to others, as well as themselves.

It's also true that no one ever caused anything to happen, intentionally or otherwise, and that, in fact, nothing that anyone ever thought happened actually did. But this can only be profoundly realized when one is past the point of using it as an excuse. Somewhere I read, "Integrity is the spine of enlightenment," and integrity begins when one accepts full responsibility for one's humanness. I cannot use awakening to excuse my behavior, and yet I am excused simply by the nature of what I really am, which is Awakeness Itself.

D.E. Harding often said, "To be saved is to be Him." Amen to that.

SUICIDE

There are more than a dozen separate buildings inside the perimeter of this prison compound, and one of them is the administration building, atop which stands a 65-foot radio tower. One morning an inmate managed to get to the roof of the administration building and then all the way to the top of the tower, where he stood precariously on a narrow metal strut.

They locked us down. They called the city fire department. They assembled a contingent of officers on the roof at the base of the tower. They brought in a ladder truck and an ambulance. They tried to talk him down, but he threatened to jump. Hours passed, and when they had to feed us lunch, they marched us single file to the chowhall and told us that if we said one word to him, they'd take us straight to the hole. At dinner when they again marched us to the chowhall he was sitting on the strut, feet dangling, a hand casually holding the antenna cable. We were in awe that he was still there, that he had with the threat of this final act brought the entire prison to a halt. He was there all day until evening when they promised not to punish him if he came down. When he did, they cuffed him and took him straight to the hole.

The next day he was in the newspaper. Some of the men in the cellhouse thought he should have jumped.

||||

Many years ago when I was in County Jail there was a man in the next cell who never spoke, never came out for showers or for recreation periods, and as far as I knew, never changed his clothes. He began to stink. He had no cellmate, and the officers avoided him, and every time I passed by his cell I'd see him sitting in the shadows on the far end of the bottom bunk.

One night I heard him gag and cough. It was the only sound I'd ever heard from him. I thought he was sick. In the morning he didn't pick up his breakfast tray. He sat on his bunk in the same place he always did, in the shadows at the back. At noon when he didn't take his lunch tray, an officer yelled at him, but he didn't respond, and at dinner when the same thing happened, the officer called a supervisor and they went in to check on him. He was sitting in his usual spot, but with one end of a black shoelace tied around his neck and the other end tied to the post of the bunk above. They said he'd been dead for a while. They said he was in jail for disorderly conduct, a misdemeanor.

Since then, three men I've known have hanged themselves with bedsheets tied to heater vents near the ceiling in their cells, and one slit his throat with a razor blade. All showed no obvious signs of depression, and one man was joking with me five minutes before he jumped off his toilet and strangled himself. I'll admit, in the early days of my sentence, I once thought of doing the same, but as it turned out I was too much of a coward to pull it off. Life seemed pointless, hopeless, an exercise in continuous embarrassment and unresolved guilt, but suicide frightened me. I told myself it was one more crime piled on top of all the others I had committed. In fact, it was murder.

||||

These days, the idea of killing myself is the ultimate absurdity, especially since discovering that what I really am can't be killed. And this body and mind—how precious "life" really is, the unspeakable grandeur of countless organisms spinning this web of presence and calling themselves "man" or "plant" or "insect," the entire world celebrating itself in a dance of infinite energy! Who would deny that? Who indeed *could* deny that?

Believe it or not, a man here tried to drown himself in his toilet, and another drank a quart of disinfectant and didn't even get sick. The base of the radio tower is now festooned with razor wire, so leaping to death is nearly impossible, and they hurry us in from the recreation yard at the mere hint of lightning, but we still might be able to electrocute ourselves if we can figure out a way to get an extension cord to the shower. And there is always the possibility of gorging our way into a heart attack, but on our meager salaries and with the dollar limit on canteen purchases, doing so could take decades. Overall, it's hard to say if there are more suicides per capita here than on the streets—probably not—but one thing is certain: There is both here and elsewhere a great lack of appreciation for what we have, for "what is," for Who we really are, manifesting as just this, just now. Anything less than the glory of that recognition is by all means suicidal.

JUST THIS

Regarding what is referred to as the Negative Way—the idea expressed by the Sanscrit term *neti neti,* "not this, not that," whereby what we think of as reality is bit by bit seen to be illusory—the fact remains that when you whittle it all away and arrive at nothing, it simultaneously explodes into everything. Despite the assertion that reality is only to be found in the storyless moment, in wholeness nothing is left out: not anything, not everything, not even nothing. The story, consisting of what appears to be a continuous thread of narrative arriving from what we imagine to be the "past" and proceeding into the "future," is as much reality as no story at all, even though it is experienced only in the present. Our imaginings are not mistakes. They are not veils of reality, they are expressions of it, and in that, they are reality, just as they appear. Like a hologram, each part reveals the all, and *is* the all.

From the point of view of No-thing, there is only empty awareness. From the point of view of Everything, there is only wholeness, awake to itself. They are not different. They are Pure Subjectivity. From the point of view of this or that, they appear as separate things, but this too is Pure Subjectivity, said to be "functioning" as this and that. This is why the only answer to the only question ever asked is: "Just this. Just this."

SPRING

It's spring, the swallows are back, and it's snowing. Two baby rabbits emerge from a hole under the sidewalk ten feet in front of my window. Tiny balls of fur, they scamper into the hole at the slightest movement. Even the swallows frighten them, and once when I knocked on the window they didn't come out for an hour.

It's the resident owls I worry about, a nighttime menace to the pigeons as well. Just last week what was left of a pigeon ended up in the dirt outside my window, and feathers floated down from the roof for days. Between the coyotes and the hawks and the owls, baby rabbits don't last long, but these two just might make it, if my banging on the window has anything to do with it.

Snowing in May, and the rabbits huddle next to the sidewalk. A six-inch lizard appears, and they bolt. Amazingly, the lizard follows them into their hole, then races out a second later. I once heard a rabbit scream, a heart-rending cry if ever there was one. It had taken refuge in the back of a Pepsi machine and got caught in the cooling fan. By the time we got it out it was a bloody mess, and it died soon after. Did my baby rabbit friends scream when the lizard appeared in their hole? Probably not. But whatever they did, the lizard was in a greater hurry coming out than going in, and it kept trucking, all the way to the cellhouse wall where I lost sight of it.

Lately the spiders have been busy on my window. I rarely see them, but every day there are more strands of silk. When the wind picks up, dirt collects on the strands and they are easy to see, so the spiders spin new ones next to the old, and by August every pane on the window is laced with brown silk. If the Health Department is due to inspect the facility, a crew comes along and blasts the windows with a high-pressure hose, and not a day later the spiders are rebuilding their webs. For spiders, this hosing must surely be the equivalent of a major tsunami, and yet they always seem to survive, and in surviving, never give up on my window.

Just now as I am writing this there is an emergency of sorts. A call for "First Responders" goes out over the PA system, and a hundred or so inmates who were coming in from the recreation yard are herded back out while the entrance door is slid shut. In a minute I know we'll be locked down, so I go to the cellhouse door to see what's up. The choking odor of pepper spray is everywhere. Outside in the main hallway there are six inmates lying face-down with their hands cuffed behind their backs, and at least two dozen officers are standing around. There is blood on the floor, a trail of it leading down the hallway, and one of the officers tells me it was a gang fight and a man was stabbed.

Back at my window, I see only one baby rabbit, and I think about the man who was stabbed and wonder if he is okay. A vine-like weed growing next to the sidewalk and partway up a fence is in full bloom, dozens of fragile pink flowers welcoming the snow. An ambulance turns into the parking lot.

THE $64,000 QUESTION

This evening I watched a documentary on PBS about particle physics. When it was over, I couldn't help but have the impression that the physicist—the observer—somehow considered himself apart, or exempt, from what was being observed. Who is this observer? If everything—all matter—is made up of subatomic particles (or "wavicles"), that "everything" includes me and the instruments I happen to be using, and if I'm using them to measure or discover myself, where is the "I" located in this equation, how do you distinguish between the observer and the observed, the subject and the object? In other words, who, or what, just wrote the above sentence? Was it the trillions of wavicles calling themselves "me," or is this "me" somehow floating above or within them, as if separate? And moreover, how is anything actually known, experienced? What is this sense of *being*, or *presence*? If I am strictly matter, how did it invent itself as a "self?" How did the observed come up with the observer?

The Dalai Lama has expressed a great deal of interest in modern science. Is it because he knows the answer that science yet ignores or denies?

THROWN TO THE WIND

In Philadelphia where I grew up I was secretly in love with the girl who lived in the big house across the street. I was twelve, and she was thirteen. Her name was Andrea. She was an only child, like me. I never saw her mother, and although I never spoke to her father, I'd see him come and go at odd hours in his black Cadillac. His face was pocked and he had slicked-back hair and he always wore a leather jacket, even with a tie. He looked like a mobster to me, and I was wary of him.

One day Andrea caught me masturbating in my garage. I was so embarrassed I ran into my house and vowed never to see her or speak to her again. I expected her father the mobster to come and kill me. I begged my parents to move, but wouldn't tell them why. For months thereafter, walking home from school I'd see Andrea who would wave and smile and try to approach me, but I would hurry by rather than face her.

As it happened, my father was transferred to the New York area that following year, and I left my shame back in that Philadelphia neighborhood I once loved. Or so I thought. In fact, as I grew older, I became increasingly embarrassed and increasingly ashamed. The most trivial affront would send me spiralling into humiliation. Although contraction had begun years before, in my teens I grew *down* with a vengeance. From the wide open and all-embracing Awareness of early childhood, I shrank to human size, to a body and mind, and in the process lost the spaciousness and fullness of my birthright. Of course, along with this loss, I learned to play the social game, to feign normalcy, but inside I was a churning swamp of emotions, not the least of which was rage.

Eventually rediscovering my spaciousness was the answer, of course. Seeing what has *always* been here— this Aware Emptiness filled with the scene—and seeing that I *am* that, opened the floodgates and drained the swamp, not all at once but enough that I was no longer poisoning myself and others. These days, things are different; that is, things and events are seen from a different point of view.

Yesterday, for instance, I went to the prison law library. There are fifteen computers for use by inmates on an appointment-only basis. We can research law, type our Motions or Opening Briefs or write letters to attorneys. The law librarian, a stern, middle-aged woman whom no one has ever seen smile, closely polices our activities and prints out our work via her own computer, and God forbid you should break any of the petty rules!

Concerning legal matters, I am a complete dummy. I am also a dummy when it comes to operating a computer, since I came to prison before personal computers were popular. In the past I would have been awash with embarrassment for being so dimwitted, so uncool, so passé as to not know where to begin, not even know how to turn the damn thing on! And then to have to repeatedly rely on others for legal advice—well, what could be worse? But here is a First-Person-Singular account of how it went:

A line forms. The older this headless, upside-down body gets, the more it seems to end up at the end of these lines, but then, why not?—it's easier to see what's coming! Now the doorway approaches as the line moves through it, and in a moment the room is within me—computers lined up on the tables to one side, the law librarian at her desk on the opposite side. Each man stops at her desk and presents his paperwork for her to view. Then it is my turn. She slides in front of me, frowning. I have her frowning face here. Amazingly, I am wearing her frowning face, and now it is asking me to empty my pockets. Looking down, I see hands turning pockets inside out, which seems appropriate because, after all, everything else is upside-down and inside out, so why not the pockets? She looks at them, then at the papers under my arm. I offer the papers to her but she waves them away and frowns at the next man in line.

The room swivels. A chair and a table approach. The computer thing sits on the table. It greets me with a blank expression. A man to my left offers to turn on the monitor—it's a flatscreen, with the button hidden on the panel edge—his hand reaching across, his finger pressing the button, his voice friendly ("It's here," he says, and I think to myself, "Yes, yes, it's *all* Here").

Memories flood in of a clerk's job I had fifteen years ago and the use of a word-processing program. I ask him for help finding the legal issues I am researching, and he scoots his chair over next to mine, then tells me what to click on, what to input, how to look up case law, statutes, rules and procedures. By the time the hour is up, I have everything required, and I am grateful for his help, for the computer, for the online publication of case law, even for the confusing legal terms I may never understand. Everything needed was given freely; if it didn't appear, it wasn't needed. Not once was there a feeling of embarrassment or of being out of place or not up to the job. And the reason is simple: There was no thing here separate from the "job," no one trying to project or protect an image of adequacy, nothing but this capacious awareness manifesting as the scene, a scene that was therefore Who I Am and All I Am, as is every scene.

Sometimes now as an old man I still think about Andrea and wonder what would have happened if I hadn't been a horny kid with my pants down in that garage. But then, what difference would it have made to her?—she seemed to think it was amusing, and before that, she seemed to think my obvious infatuation with her was amusing. As for me, well, I could rummage in my psyche for years and perhaps come up with several semi-rational reasons why I experienced such a severe case of embarrassment, back then and on into adulthood, but the root of the problem was that at that stage of my life, I had finally bought the lie of individuality and was already paying for it. I had, in effect, sold my soul to the concept of self and other, packaged it in this bag of skin and closed out the world, believing I was for myself what others made of me from where they were, which was a singular and limited speck in a vast vast universe, one-hundred-percent human.

Thank God I've been cracked open, thrown to the wind. Thank God for this gift of freedom. And Who else is there to thank, when you come down to it? God and the gift are one. That is why gratitude's other name is bliss.

YOU ARE NOT IN THE WORLD, THE WORLD IS IN YOU

It's a fact. Seeing it is believing it, and once seen, nothing is the same. You are the center of the universe, a universe that is entirely within you, that comes from you, that *is* you. Seeing the world inside you, all is sanctified. Everything, every object, every being, is suddenly made holy, is seen as an expression of the love that you are.

A neighbor here is apparently in the throes of a midlife crisis. He sighs loudly and often, rarely smiles, and from time to time erupts in fits of anger or frustration, shouting obscenities at no one in particular. He says the world is closing in on him, that life is hardly worth living. He blames the government, the prison system, his job, his boss, his cellmate, his family on the outside, and on rare occasions, even himself.

To him, of course, "himself" is a separate being located in a body "over here," while "out there" is the troublesome world made up of other beings, objects, and events that he must manipulate in order to get what he desires or avoid what he doesn't. In his case, he is either a poor manipulator or the world has decided to beat him into submission, as evidenced by the fact that he's a first-class loser, and a sore one at that.

Then I discovered that every Sunday he goes to church, and according to others who know him, that God is the only person or thing he never complains about.

Somehow he has made God exempt from all that he perceives to be wrong with the world, even though God created it, even though God *is* it.

Whenever things get iffy, whenever doubts creep in or problems arise, I like to remind myself that I'm not in the world, the world is in me. So one day I decided to relate this to my troubled neighbor, particularly since at that moment he happened to be standing in front of me, appearing Here in this Awake Empty Space, and therefore, he was all I could claim *I* was: a first-class loser.

His reply was a harangue about how I should mind my own business, and when I said I thought I was, he grew quiet and looked down at his shoes and I could feel the air between us boiling with rage. I thought he was going to hit me, but instead, before he walked off, he quietly told me to leave him alone.

Which was my lesson for the day. Leave him alone, leave it all alone, just as it is. There never was and never will be a world in him, because it's all Here, appearing and disappearing in this great Now—which, in his case, happens to be God pretending to be other, complaining about Himself.

DREAMS

When I was a teenager I used to dream about a girl with long blond hair and blue eyes and a Hollywood tan who, no matter what the circumstances, would start out being attracted to me but would soon lose interest, and then sometimes would even morph into someone or something vaguely ominous or outright dreadful.

And then one day I met her. After my first marriage but before my second I happened to be in Canada, up to no good as usual, when I was introduced to a Scandinavian girl named Inga who charmed me with outrageous stories of her young life as the daughter of a spy, growing up in such exotic-sounding places as Istanbul and Bombay. A week later when she took me home to meet her parents, they insisted the four of us go ballroom dancing that night. Inga borrowed a jacket and tie from her father for me, then popped a tab of LSD in both of our mouths, and off we went for what turned out to be one of the worst evenings of my life, two hours of undulating walls and neon food, followed by a hellish eternity of the foxtrot on drugs. Later that night after her parents had gone to bed, she led me to her father's den which was crammed with radio equipment: transmitters and receivers and other electronics I couldn't name. I was awed. Maybe he really was a spy! Inga wanted to make love on his leather couch, but I was wary of hidden cameras and expected at any second to hear coded gibberish blurt from the radio.

Despite her clawing, in my fractured state this was no place for passion, and I had the feeling that the sooner I left that house the sooner I would wake up to reality.

The following week we drove north and spent three days camping on an island in the middle of the clearest, cleanest lake I had ever seen. It was another sort of dream, one filled with quartz cliffs and unlimited skies and the call of loons. We explored by canoe, cooked bass over an open fire, drank lake water from our hands, wore clothes only when we neared the shore where the mosquitoes were. This was the dream you don't want to end but know it soon will, if only because you won't be able to stand another minute of perfection. When we drove back to Toronto and I dropped her off at her apartment, she smiled in a way that said it was over, and the only thing I could think at the time was that I'd never find out if her father was a spy, and who for.

Lately I've been thinking about how one dream ends and another begins, at times so seamlessly you can't tell them apart. Sometimes early in the morning I really *can't* tell, and whereas it used to scare me a little, now a night dream might flow into a day dream in the same way one might walk from one muliplex theater to the next through an adjoining door. Often my night dreams are bizarre, but there are few that make as little sense as this one I am having now, the pen scribbling out words that arrive unbidden from God-knows-where, the Great Mystery gabbing first about apparent events in Its so-called "past," and now about Itself from within Itself. How and why are there dreams at all, this one included? And without them, what would Nothing be like, this same Nothing that sings the song of everything?

Several days after Inga had dumped me, my partner and I discovered we were under surveillance by the RCMP, Canada's FBI, and the two of us barely made it out of town with our freedom. Inga, as it turned out, had to have been the "spy," and we knew who for. Some dreams keep showing up, whether or not you wish they wouldn't.

Somewhere I read recently that when you wake up in the morning, you never blame a character in your dream for causing harm; to do so would be the height of absurdity. And why? Because it was all in your head, purely a fabrication of mind!

For a long time I blamed Inga for betraying me. After I left Canada I learned that she'd been busted on a minor drug charge shortly before we'd met, and that she'd fingered me as part of a deal to avoid jail. So in my mind she was a rat, and I let everyone know it.

But in those days what I failed to realize was that Inga and I were both characters in this great dream had by No One, that this No One is Pure Consciousness, and Pure Consciousness is the only dreamer of every dream, night and day alike (although we call the latter "reality").

Furthermore, what I am—what "I AM" *is*—is this same Pure Consciousness, manifesting as everyone and everything, all that appears *within* and *as* these so-called dreams, every nighttime and daytime story ever dreamed up. What I am is the Alone, Pure Consciousness, and failing then to see that, I blamed Inga, and whenever I identify with the character "me," whenever I am dissatisfied with the scene that presents itself and wish it were other than what it is, I am the Alone forgetting what I am, forgetting that there is no one and no thing in the dream that is *not* what I am, which is Pure Consciousness.

And now of course it occurs to me that even if Inga's father *was* a spy, I know who for. In these moments, I can't help but be amazed—awe and wonder seem not to be optional—and gratitude pours forth from "no other" to all that is "other," a mystery I Alone couldn't do without.

NO MOTIVE

Attached to the cellhouse is a building that houses the Operations Center, with several staff offices inside. Most of the offices are architectural afterthoughts, drywall boxes slapped together some thirty years after the original structure was built.

One day a swallow flew in the Operations Center door as an officer was walking out. It hovered near the ceiling, and then began fluttering from wall to wall, chirping—back and forth until finally it perched on one of the box roofs, exhausted. The officers propped the door open and tried to shoo it toward the entrance with a broom, but the bird simply hopped to the roof of another office. Eventually a ladder was produced, but each time an officer would climb the ladder, the swallow would move to a new location. Finally, after a phone call and the arrival of several more officers from other parts of the prison, a dozen inmates were summoned, each with a bedsheet, and within a half hour and much ado, the swallow was cornered by a phalanx of sheets and gave up.

An inmate named Savage lovingly carried it outside and set it free, but it was still too weak to fly, so he placed it on a ledge eight feet off the ground and walked away. Minutes later, the swallow took off, and everyone cheered.

That same day, I heard on the radio that a man had walked into a restaurant and shot five people dead, then turned the gun on himself. No motive could be determined.

GET PHYSICAL

They say that waking up is not a conceptual event, not something that happens through the use of the intellect, although the intellect may lead one to what has been termed the "gateless gate." This is because awakening is non-conceptual. It is prior to concepts. It is that aware space in which a concept forms, lasts for however long, and then vanishes, to be replaced by yet another concept. Thus, awareness is the core, the ground of every concept. In fact, it is the ground of everything that appears and disappears within it moment by moment—every thought, every thing. It is what we really are—Pure Awareness, appearing as every thought and every thing—and profoundly realizing this is said to be "waking up" to our true identity.

A Buddhist friend asked me what I thought "awakening" was, and the above was more or less my answer. He looked at me as if I'd been barking, or maybe speaking Chinese. Explaining what enlightenment is is one thing; understanding it is another. And neither the explaining nor the understanding have anything to do with being it, except perhaps as yet another expression of it, another passing thought, another passing thing.

The irony is, enlightenment is ultra-physical. It is actual. It is intensely intimate. You cannot be more of what you are than What You Really Are. It is Pure Subjectivity, and *everything* is that. *You* are Pure Subjectivity, and everything is What You Are. How much more physical could it be?

Which is perhaps why so many have such great difficulty accepting the ease and simplicity of What They Really Are. Buried in concepts, believing what they have been told they are from day one, it is indeed a fearful thing to embrace the radical fact of one's true nature.

For instance, when a sage says you are Stillness Itself, do you actually experience being completely still, while the world moves within you? Walking, are you at rest while the earth flows past, legs striding to keep up? Driving, are you motionless while telephone poles and buildings and the landscape whiz by? Turning, is it the room or the houses or the mountains that turn, and not you? Looking at looking, looking back at what you are looking out of, do you see the empty and boundless and motionless Awareness that you are, what Aristotle referred to when he said that God is the "unmoved mover of the world"?

And when a sage declares that you are the "Ground" of the universe, do you actually see that you are literally the foundation of the world, the bottomless source of all that is and has its being "up there"? Looking back, do you see the frameless awake window that you are, infinitely high and low and wide and into which all that is, anything and everything, fits with ease? Taking the top of the window as "up" and the bottom as "down," are you not the base, the ground, of all that appears? Appearing Here, the only place anything can possibly appear, is not the world presented vertically? Even your body, feet to shoulders—is it not clearly upside-down? And where you thought(!) you had a head, on present evidence, isn't there nothing but this Aware Nothing, wide awake and luminous and at the seat of all being?

And when a sage points out that you are The Alone, do you see, actually see, another Awareness anywhere else? Is it possible that there *isn't* another Awareness, that there cannot be two Awarenesses (or even one), considering that it is empty, void, no-thing at all? Is it not present only Here—as the One Presence, and like space, big enough and roomy enough for all to share?

On present evidence, then, being in the now-moment, do you see that you are Stillness Itself, that you are the Ground, and that you are The Alone? If so, then you see What You Really Are. And if not, if there is resistance—then there may be confusion, there may be suffering, but you are still What You Really Are.

TARANTULA

And then there was the year of the great tarantula migration. They were everywhere, crossing the sidewalks, climbing the cellhouse walls, pawing through the grass on the lawns. Only once previously had I seen so many tarantulas: thousands upon thousands crossing a highway in the Mexican desert, so many the road was black, their bodies crunching under the tires of my van.

What is it about tarantulas that makes them so gentle, so seemingly open to human contact? I watched an officer pluck one from the cellhouse wall and place it in his lunch bag; the spider never raised its fangs and seemed blithely content among the sandwiches and bottles of water. The officer said he was taking it home for his daughter.

This was the first time I had allowed a spider to crawl on me. (Growing up, I had been seriously afraid of them, and avoided them or killed them without compunction.) An inmate named Josh, a cellhouse grounds keeper, approached me with one in his hand. He gently coaxed it onto mine, and immediately it began to crawl up my arm, slowly, feeling its way, each of its eight legs ever-so-lightly, almost reverently, caressing my skin, up to the sleeve of my tee shirt where I then placed my other hand for it to continue on.

To say that I was fascinated by this extraordinary creature is an understatement. I was transfixed, watching it crawl first up one arm and then the other, as if it had hypnotized me with its multiple eyes which all the while were, I was certain, fixed upon me, as though it were studying me, wondering what to make of the extraordinary creature that offered it hand after hand and arm after arm upon which to climb. Eventually it stopped, and I prodded it onto a wall where it remained for some time, where we watched each other from this same primordial emptiness—not the same emptiness that we *shared*, but the same emptiness that we *were*.

And all that day and the days that followed, not once did I see an officer or an inmate kill one. Mostly, they observed them with great interest. (Later that week I happened to watch a nature show on TV about meerkats, and in one scene a half-dozen or so were standing upright intensely studying a snake that had approached their burrow—a scene I had witnessed repeatedly all over the prison grounds vis-à-vis humans and tarantulas!) Perhaps it is fascination with creatures we are hardwired to avoid, or simply that we so seldom see them in our midst. Or perhaps it is because we prisoners have been scratched from the race of life and now have the time and the inclination to notice what is here, what lives all around us, what, in our hearts, we are all made of.

RAGS TO RICHES

In Costa Rica I met a woman in a whore house who refused to have sex with me because I was plastered. I liked her, so I paid her anyway, then later told my friends I had sex with her three times.

In Chile I went to the ritziest brothel in Santiago. Even though I had a pocketful of cash, I refused to pay the house price, and instead lost my money in a drunken stupor on the street outside.

In Monterey, Mexico, a friend and I paid for sex with phony traveller's checks, and the next morning I swore I had hit bottom. Then a week later I woke up in a mud puddle at five a.m. in a red light district in Mazatlan, and to this day I have no idea how I got there.

Sadly, this isn't half of how bad it got. What drove me to this personal hell? What spawns such degradation and violence, not only mine but all the human cruelty we see and hear about every day of our lives? What brings on such rampant greed and bickering for power? How could innocent and loving children grow up to be monsters of rape and war?

The answer is that, not knowing any better and unable to keep anything out, we believe a message taught to us when we are very young, and that message is: "You are what you look like to others." One simple message conveyed to each of us by our parents, our siblings, our friends, our society—that I am an object, one among seven billion similar objects, but separate, intrinsically existing as an individual self. Such a seemingly innocuous and innocent message, and for the rest of our lives we are mired in a body and possessed by a mind, alienated from a world we feel powerless to control, hopelessly insignificant in the face of a universe too vast to conceive.

Unless we are lucky. Unless, maybe, we are backed into a corner so dark there is no choice but to seek the light. Unless we are propelled by a yearning so strong we cannot let go until we are free.

Recently I read an article about several miscreants during the Buddha's time, one in particular named Angulimala who was a serial killer until he woke up in the Buddha's presence, and I thought, "Thank God I'm not as bad as him!"

But is that true? Every time I think I am this separate self and not this Awake Emptiness that is my true nature, I am living the lie, perpetrating a mortal sin. Multiply that by the world's population, and especially when nations live that lie, our planet becomes a dangerous place. But how do we stop? Where do we begin?

What I have learned is that we start by seeing Who We Really Are, actually looking and seeing, and in doing so we come to accept who we seem to be. Our Buddhist teacher said something during our last monthly meeting that struck me as profoundly relevant to my situation, to the shame and guilt that plagued me in the past and that perhaps we all suffer from in our lives from time to time, if for no other reason than for the "original sin" of our mistaken belief in separation. He said, "Don't be ashamed of who you are." An obvious statement, but he meant, Don't be ashamed of your ego, of the separate self you think you are, because it is natural, it is *lila*, it is part of the great drama of appearance, all the parts of which are actually played by the Awake Emptiness that you really are. It is Who You Are, manifesting as who you seem to be, and for that reason it is okay; in fact, it is far more than okay, it is the One functioning as two, love in action, the manifestation of Compassion Itself.

And then I realized that he may also have meant it in another way: "Don't be ashamed of Who You Are." Because, especially in this environment, too often I am reticent, even when asked, to explain what is meant by a passage in a book or to point to what is true, reticent even to show others how to point at the Awake Emptiness at their core, to help them discover the No-thing they are. Don't be ashamed of Who You Are, despite the ridicule or scorn, because Who You Are is what everything is.

Either way, it was good advice, and I took it gratefully.

Later, he asked me how seeing and being Who I Really Am (one's "Basic Goodness," as he put it) made a difference in life, and specifically in the ability to love and act compassionately toward others. I said that it made all the difference in the world, that the change is so radical that, although everything may appear as it did before, what was previously seen from the point of view of a separate self is one hundred percent the opposite of the way things really are. Instead of a "me" here and everyone else over there, everyone is inside this Awake Emptiness that I am, and is therefore an aspect of Who I Am. Instead of an imagined object here (me) confronted by a perceived object there (you), as Emptiness I am open for you, I welcome you, I disappear in your favor—I see no ego, not even a face here with which to keep you out; I am invaded by you in a relationship that is a relationship of One, an indescribable intimacy experienced only by this Emptiness that, because of you, because of the world that appears within this Emptiness, is in fact Emptiness/Fullness, Oneness, an intimacy that alone is the true meaning of love. Love and compassion flourish naturally, effortlessly. In fact, love and compassion are what this Awake Emptiness *is*.

In prison, alcohol and sex are illegal, but not hard to find if you look. Fortunately, I have been without either for thirty-some years, at first because I seemingly willed it so, and later because the tendencies to harm myself and others had dropped away. When I first came to prison I remember thinking, "Without the debauchery, what will I do? Who will I be?" It actually worried me. The old line, "Been down so long it looks like up" was my reality. Who would I be if I couldn't sabotage myself and then take it out on others?

The answer, although it came some years later, turned out to be "No one," a surprise then and a surprise every time I repeat it. It's so radical it's mind-blowing, so freeing and so entirely permeated with love it's delicious. And impossible to explain. Life became miraculous. The desire to care for it became paramount. Everything is internal, all of creation, and the astonishment of that fact spilled over into everyday deeds. This was how seeing Who I Really Am made a difference, and although the seeing never changes—Emptiness is always empty, always awake, always capacity for whatever fills it—the meaning and appreciation of it bloom and continue to flower as the apparent years go by.

EVOLUTION

At the heart of what I am—indeed, that which I am in its entirety—is pure unalloyed Consciousness, appearing as this and that, anything and everything. All is Consciousness and Consciousness is all. There is only Consciousness: uncreated, undying, underlying only Itself.

Since as Consciousness I am all things, think of how elastic I am! I appear as anything, and anything I appear as is elastic to the core.

Take this First Person upside-down headless body, for instance. It can "grow" the appendage it needs until it no longer needs it, then shed it. Right now this hand has grown a pen so that this body can write about itself, and earlier it grew a broom, a mop, a dustpan and various rags with which to clean an office, an office that also happens to be what I am.

And it isn't only small items it evolves. Years ago this First Person body routinely strapped a car to itself and "ran" at 60 miles per hour, and quite often it grew a commercial airliner with which to fly great distances. Once, having grown to the size of a ship, it "swam" in the Pacific until it made itself seasick, and after un-growing the ship, it grew a motorhome and became a house on the road. There seems no end to what it can do or undo, even though it may not yet know how to evolve it. Odd that we humans think that evolution ends where flesh does, and that our tools and inventions are not extensions of our selves. In Oneness, what could be separate from what? Where could my body end and something else begin?

And what about our larger body, the planet? Is the planet conscious? Of course! I am Consciousness Itself, and the planet, like my human body, is an appearance of that. It too evolves what it needs, such as telescopes and probes with which to see its planetary sisters, the Internet with which to provide itself a brain. On a planetary time scale, in which the history of humanity is only a moment, there is no telling what the future holds in terms of evolutionary possibilities, via us or via other life forms, and at any planetary moment it may undo any or all of it, if the need arises, as may our larger bodies the solar system and galaxy. My true body is the universe, and ultimately it is the universe which evolves the universe, and every bit of it is what I am in continuous flux.

So the next time you iron a shirt or mow the lawn or take the train to work, notice your astounding flexibility. Slip on a bicycle and grow wheels when you need them, or strap on a Cessna and soar like a hawk. Grow a winter coat when it's cold, or swim like a fish in the summer with your scuba gear. Take nothing for granted, for it's all what you are, every astonishing particle of it dancing your dance. How magnificently creative you are!

LOCKDOWN

Today we are locked down. Considering the way the usual routine was so abruptly interrupted and the fact that all inmates were called in from their work stations, this one feels like it will last awhile, maybe a week or two. The rumor going around is that two female guards in another facility were attacked by an inmate, and one was killed. I pray this isn't true, but God knows it's happened before, and when it does, every prison in the state locks down until the staff can sort out what took place and how to prevent it from happening again.

Just now the TV news confirms the worst. My cellmate sighs and shakes his head. I think of the officer, and wonder about her family, how devastated they must be. I think of all the other officers and the stress they endure, knowing it could happen to them. I think of their sorrow and their anger and how they view us, how a tragic incident like this only widens the gulf between "us" and "them."

I think about the inmate who did it. I wonder how he feels, what he'll tell himself at night before he sleeps, if he'll sleep at all. I think about how he'll spend the rest of his life locked in solitary on death row, no doubt on the same tier with the last inmate who murdered a guard. God save us from this violence we cannot control at the hands of our own ignorance. Sometimes the sadness floods my heart. I drown in it. Inside I feel I know what it's like to be killed. It's in my bones. It drives the joy from my being, then strangely, welcomes it back transformed into love. I can't say how. I don't know why. That any of this is here, even if it is the result of my own doing, confounds me to the core.

RUNAWAY TRAIN

Sometimes I long for a normal life. Sometimes I wish I were a regular guy living in a middle-class neighborhood with a regular wife, two cars and an RV in the driveway, and two kids who argue all day except when we all eat dinner or watch a movie together, which never happens.

And I almost had it. In Hawaii a year out of college I married into a good family. There was a traditional church wedding and a reception at a private club in Waikiki for a hundred well-wishers, including a Hollywood star. My parents flew in from New York. My dad and I golfed, my mother and fiancée shopped. We were showered with gifts, and after a week at a fancy hotel on Maui for our honeymoon, we started our lives together in a three-bedroom ranch with a double garage, directly across the street from the Chief of Police.

Of course, I blew it. I caught "rock fever," as they say, bored driving in circles around an island I couldn't leave. I fought with my wife, I hated her dogs, I was tired of the beach. It was as if something were rotting inside me, and no matter what I did, it only got worse. A year later we divorced, and by then the counter-culture of the '60s was in full swing and I fell head first into the fray.

When I look back to my freshman and sophomore years in college, I see the innocent dreams I knew even then wouldn't come true. I joined the Air Force R.O.T.C.

because I wanted to become a fighter pilot, then wore red socks just to piss off the Colonel. I thought of becoming a salesman like my dad, then drove a garbage truck during the summer months between semesters. I chose psychology as a major with the idea that I could eventually sort out the mess in my head, then buried myself in football and drank myself into a haze every weekend. I got engaged three times to three different girls, with the same ring. I wanted to be somebody, but didn't know who.

Oddly, after transferring from that rural college to a big city university, my junior and senior years were entirely different. My grades were up and football was gone. I met a girl I didn't get engaged to. I worked after classes in an ice cream store to pay my rent, joined the French Club and drifted toward the arts. I was a square living among the Beats. Kerouac and Ginsberg were the rage, and then by the middle of my senior year I could feel myself unraveling again, this time caught between the Sinatra of my parents and the Dylan of my peers but sliding toward the streets of New York and an unknown I deeply feared.

I'd like to say that after graduation I chose Hawaii because I wanted to straighten out my life and make something of myself, but the truth is that, out of all the graduate schools I applied to, Hawaii was the only one that accepted me. Despite the fact that my teaching assistantship was cancelled after I arrived, for awhile the move to the islands was yet another respite from my propensity to self-destruct. I found a part-time job as a teacher, got married to the aforementioned girl from a good family, and started a new life as a regular guy in a middle-class neighborhood. But oh, how quickly it was over! A trip to the mainland, the divorce, and then back to Oahu and into the hippie life in old Waikiki, looking for a way out of someone I wasn't.

In retrospect it's obvious I was never in charge. I certainly never wanted to make a career out of breaking the law. They teach us here that we need to make the right choices, but how do we do that as someone we're not? Most of us appear to follow the tracks laid down by society, but some of us are runaway trains, bound for nowhere, and too often that nowhere is nowhere good.

It amazes me now, seeing the way this all played out. How many slaps in the face does one need before they realize they don't have a face? How many attempts at "normal" does one make before they know that "normal" is a lie? And how long does it take before one sees that a "regular" life is irregular to the core; is, as some would say, the definition of "insane"?

And the craziest thing of all is that, not often but from time to time, I long for the lie and find moments of comfort in the dream of separation. But not for long, thank God, not for long. For soon after, whatever longing there is turns to angst, whatever comfort to dis-ease, and, unlike years ago when I responded with destructive behavior and others were hurt, now the journey is short and quick and the destination is home—my true home—right here where I have always been, where peace and freedom lie and where all is cherished as Who I Really Am. These days, the runaway train barely leaves the station, and although the destination is still nowhere, thank God it is all nowhere good.

GONE

Today a close friend was transferred to another prison. We'd lived in the same area for twelve years, ate our meals together, worked together, cracked each other up with the same weird humor. Now he's gone, and like most of the men who leave here, I'll probably never see him again.

So today I'm blue. All morning I've had episodes of post-ventricular contractions—skipped heartbeats—strange flutterings in my chest that seem all too appropriate for the occasion.

Outside the window, rain collects in broad puddles, and the sky hangs heavy and lifeless. At work I sink into the usual routine: push a broom, sling a mop, clean the staff toilet. Officers come and go, and one stops to say how good a worker my friend was and how much they'll miss him.

Later, in the cellhouse, my cellmate tells me I'm wearing a long face. "Thank God I can't see it," I reply, and he smiles. The TV is on, there's coffee in the carafe, a crossword puzzle sits on the metal desk. The dayroom quickly fills with men coming in from morning work crews, and there is the usual banter, cards being shuffled at the tables, dominos clacking, laughter. A song on a distant radio triggers a memory of my wife.

It's one of those days, gloriously sad, and I find myself open, embracing the hollow in my gut, humbled by the persistence of this tenderness, this vulnerability, this empty and yet all-consuming presence.

ASSUME THAT!

A friend said to me one day when we had assumed something that turned out not to be true, "You know what the definition of 'assume' is?"

"Tell me," I said.

"To make an ass out of u and me."

Probably an old joke, but just the same, true to the bone.

And what if we never assumed anything, but took the moment exactly as it was presented, shorn of memory, shorn of what we'd learned or been told by others? What would that be like?

For instance, what does your body look like from where you are? Isn't it, in any position (but easiest to see when you are sitting or lying down), upside-down and headless, totally unlike those other bodies you see "over there"? Isn't your body the only body in the world that appears that way, and if so, has the meaning of that perhaps escaped you?

If what you see above your chest is empty space and not a head, isn't it curious that everything in the present scene, no matter how large (a room or an expanse of sky or a hundred miles of mountain range) fits easily within that space, and in such a way that you can say that the space and the scene are one and the same? And isn't the space/scene awake, and awake to itself? Though there is nothing there, can you deny that it is What You Are, here and now? Why assume you are in a body when it's obvious that the body is in What You Are, which is Awake Empty Space? How could it be otherwise?

Furthermore, do you see or have you ever seen another awakeness, another awareness or consciousness, anywhere else in the world? If not, why assume there *is* another; why take it for granted that so-called "others" each possess (or are possessed by) a separate consciousness, one that is other than the one you see right where you are? How could there be multiples of empty space, of nothingness?

And when you see others walk or run or otherwise move through the scene, why assume that you do also? Looking at the awake empty space above your chest, looking at looking, how could you move when you're no-thing, when there's nothing that *could* move? All that appears—anything and everything, all of time and space—moves within you, and you are Stillness Itself, prior to all of time and space, that in which all of time and space appear. Why assume you're the body moving through the scene when it's obvious—and visibly so— that the scene moves through you?

Where is it that you experience anything? Is it here, or is it over there? Even science demonstrates that everything you experience is experienced where you are and not someplace else. Why, then, when you can plainly see and hear and feel that everything is experienced where you are, why assume that anything is "over there"? Is it not obviously all here, right where it's seen or heard or felt? Is there even such a place as "there"? How would you ever know?

We assume we fall into a state of dreamless sleep at night when actually we experience nothing of the sort.

We assume we are born and we die even though we have never been a "thing" that could do so. We assume a car is a car or a tree is a tree because we have named them so, but what are they really in their essence, in the immediacy of the moment, before memory and thought? What really are all objects, appearing here in this awake empty space, including human beings, including the upside-down headless body you assumed you were but see you are not?

In fact, there is only one thing that can be assumed because it can always be seen, always be experienced, and that is the Experiencer, No-thing filled with Everything, Awake Empty Space manifesting as the "ten thousand things." If we must assume something, why not assume that? After all, it is all that is.

JUST ANOTHER STORY

Allow me to swagger a bit. Forgive me if I indulge in this "self" I once so ferociously touted as all-too-real. After all, we've all had our greatest moments, our finest hour, and this was my ticket to the stars!

You see, I escaped from prison. It was a maximum security federal prison in Mexico where I had been serving time for drug-running, and I walked out the front gate dressed as an attorney on a Sunday afternoon and onto a city street under a brilliant April sky with tears streaming down the makeup on my cheeks, scot-free, as simple as that.

When I got to the States, I called my wife and she fainted. And then three months later she left me for another man, a friend who had bought the ranch I owned before I went to prison. I missed her. I had paid so little attention to her that I couldn't blame her for leaving, but I missed her anyway.

So I gathered a crew, four women and two men, and went back to Mexico and broke out my partner and three of his friends from that same maximum-security federal prison, scot-free, as simple as that.

What I've not said is that my partner and his friends had been tunneling for six months, inch by inch with a spoon and a pillow case, under two thirty-foot walls and all the way to the street outside where we were parked in a van. And up from the hole they came, scot-free, as simple as that.

We were heroes to some, villains to others. There were front page headlines. There was talk of a movie deal. All that had ever gone wrong had suddenly come right. In one climactic moment, we were remade in the eyes of those who knew us. We were back, we were clean, we were free.

And in the end, after the celebration, I was miserable. Miserable because I figured it would never again get as good as that, never get any better than that moment, and the moment was not only gone, it was hollow to begin with. Even now, the story is hollow in the telling of it. It was, and is, just another story, another distraction, a diversion from what, if I had only known then, was the real breakout, the escape to what I've been all along—this magnificent nothing, aware of everything.

The value of it, I suppose, is that it reminds me of the futility of my search for fulfillment in the world, as if I were separate from it and could somehow reap from it an advantage.

It is laughable to think that I could ever have considered myself free. Free from what? Myself? Free from that which I already am—freedom itself? Years ago I tacked a note to my bulletin board that read, "There is no escape from life. It is what you are." And that's that. We—all of us—are scot-free, as simple as that.

Ah but these stories! Even though they are hollow, even though nothing ever happened, are they not our finest moments, each one told with the smile of recognition from this place of no-place, of stillness, of nothing ever told?

UNCONDITIONAL LOVE

Today an officer told me the definition of unconditional love. He said, "If you lock your spouse and your dog in the trunk of a car and come back two hours later and open it, which one will be happy to see you?"

I can't imagine anyone putting that to a test, but the point made is that there are few among us who practice unconditional love. Lock me in the trunk of a car with your dog, I won't be the one wagging a tail when you open it!

Depending, that is, on where I'm coming from. Suppose I don't take myself for a spouse? Or for that matter, a person? Asking the question, "What am I?" and answering it by looking at what is looking, suppose I see nothing, that is, no-thing except this awake empty space for things to appear in? How would it go when you open the trunk and I see your face, the sky, your dog wagging its tail, all *inside* of this awake space, a space which is, once seen, undoubtedly What I am?

When there is nobody home, when you disappear in favor of another, when you die so that others may live within you, that alone is unconditional love. No "person-to-person," no "others," no relationship. Only self-giving love, a love that is all about them, a "them" that is all you can be said to "be," for you—who you thought you were as a "spouse" or a "person"—that separate one has vanished.

Ask your dog!

EDDIE

My mother's name was Eddie. Not Edie, but Eddie. And oddly, she passed through the world, at least my world, as an eddy, a current barely noticed in the flood of my father's presence.

She was born into a working-class family in Philadelphia. During the Great Depression she and my dad took in laundry to pay the bills, but after that, all during the war and during my school years, she did volunteer work, mostly accounting, for one charity after another.

I remember her then as freckled, overweight, and blithely obedient to my dad except on those rare occasions when she shared a martini with him before supper, the only time I ever saw her assert herself. She was never angry. Her passivity embarrassed me, especially in front of my friends. She was maddeningly quiet, the epitome of the 1950s housewife and martyr, and I can't remember a time during those early years when I didn't feel guilty in her presence.

She tried. I think I confused her with my deviousness and unwillingness to accept her love. She smothered me with it, held me in what for her must have been a painful embrace, an only child she clung to all the more because he rebelled.

In the '60s after my divorce in Hawaii, she fell ill. Problems were never discussed in my family; if anything, they were denied or repressed. And so I never knew she'd had a mastectomy a decade earlier during my college years, never knew until long after the cancer had returned and spread to her liver. And then, strangely, she became larger than the life I had assigned to her, larger at least than my dad.

By then I was living in a Colorado ski town with the woman who would eventually become my second wife, a year before my daughter was born. Reluctantly, I invited my mother to spend a week with us—my mother never swore, rarely drank, and never in my entire life had I heard her say the words "drugs" or "sex," while my soon-to-be wife was a pot-smoking acid head from LA with a penchant for bad language and nudity in front of her countless hippie friends. When I met my mother at the airport in Denver, I was half-drunk and two hours late, and I found her standing alone in an empty baggage area with her suitcase at her side. She was a waif, half her former size, her grey hair spiky and thinned by chemo, looking lost and more than a little forlorn, even after she'd spotted me walking toward her.

I can't explain what happened to her in that ski town. I'm not sure if she approved of the beard I had grown or the run-down miner's cabin we'd rented or the boisterous woman I lived with who took her in and made her feel more important and appreciated than I ever could have, but my mother came alive. Maybe it was the thin air, or the pot smoke in that tiny house, or the wild Jeep ride above tree line in the mountains, or maybe it was simply the freedom of being away from my father for those few days, her last days on earth, as it were, a final fling for a woman who had lived most of her life in a nun-like cocoon.

She drank wine. She tried pot. She laughed and posed for pictures with our hippie friends. She helped with the meals and did the dishes and chatted with my crazy significant other like a teenage girl, and when she left, she was not my mother.

Some months later I flew to New York and saw her in the hospital just before she died. She smiled, and when I took her hand, I broke down. All those years of being embarrassed, of being ashamed of her, and there she was, more beautiful in her last moments than I had ever seen her. We cried together, and she got sick, and the nurse came in, and my father wanted to leave, and suddenly I was furious with him, and furious with the nurse who was flirting with me instead of caring for my mother, and furious at the crappy room with no view that my mother was dying in, furious with the whole shitty game of life that everyone except my mother was still playing.

At the funeral I refused to ride in the limousine with my dad. Instead, I drove my mother's car at the rear of the procession. During the wake, he said something I never forgave him for, at least not until I saw him years later during my last visit with him when he met his granddaughter. He said if he could have done it all over again, he would have married a stronger woman. Perhaps he said it for my benefit, knowing how as a child I had recoiled from her love. Or maybe he just couldn't admit to himself how much he missed her. One thing seemed certain: He never knew who the weak ones were in our little three-person family.

Many years later my brother-in-law sent some photos he'd received from my dad's second wife after he died. One was of my mother and me at the beach in New Jersey. In it, I am four or five years old, wearing an "Our

Gang" beanie festooned with buttons, and there is a toy bucket and shovel in my lap. My mother sits next to me in the sand, leaning on one freckled arm. She is smiling—beaming—and behind her is the blue Atlantic, as far as you can see.

VIOLENCE

Occasionally there are fights in the chowhall, and the problem with fights in the chowhall is that not only are fists thrown, sometimes food trays are also. Jacob, a friend who recently lost his head and discovered the world in its place, last week also discovered in its place a plate of beans, two hot dog buns and two turkey franks with mustard, all while sitting peacefully at a table and minding his own business. A man at the next table, angry with another man over something said, had pitched his tray as a prelude to battle, and Jacob got the brunt of the toss. And rather than get upset or get involved himself, he calmly moved to another table where I happened to be sitting, and we spent the remaining time chatting about headlessness and the Perennial Philosophy, Jacob with mustard on his ear and beans tangled in his hair. If on my last day I have forgotten all else, surely I'll remember the joy of that special moment, the two of us but One Spirit, open for whatever appeared, calm in the midst of the chaos.

Lately this prison feels like it's going to explode. I've seen it before. During my stay in that Mexican prison, on a Sunday when my wife and kids were visiting in the cellblock, a full-scale riot broke out, 500 angry men with sticks and shanks, setting fire to anything that would burn. There were only nine of us Americans, and we managed to barricade ourselves and our visitors inside a cellblock to wait it out. The police arrived. The Mexican Army arrived. Soldiers stood atop the walls with automatic weapons, and eventually the rioters returned to their cellblocks and the visitors were able to leave.

I can't imagine how much worse it would be if it happened here, 1700 men boiling with rage, mob rule gone mad. I know the feeling. For years, anger filled my days, fueled my every move, no matter how I tried to suppress it or smooth it over so that it looked like something else. I blamed others, I blamed the government, I blamed everything, often for a reason that made no sense. Sometimes it felt like my life was an ongoing riot, and tragically I was too much of a coward to see why, refusing to accept what eventually I had to: that the fault lay with no one else, that the ignorance would be found nowhere but here.

And now it's all around me, a daily reminder of the volcano I once was. The difference is that it no longer defines me. Sometimes it floats through this Emptiness as a subtle feeling, a vibe, and sometimes it flares up and clatters through with bared teeth, but no longer does it reside here. Truth won't allow it.

Which is not to say it is avoided. On the contrary, it is a matter of embracing that which appears, even embracing the resistance to that which appears. I've no doubt that, in my case, the path to Emptiness began well before my involvement in any traditional path, Buddhist or otherwise. It began in angst, was fueled by fear, and finally came to fruition in desperation. Even if there were such a thing as individual choice, I had none. And this is true of many seekers, I believe, for when you spend a good portion of your life in emotional pain or inflicting emotional pain upon others, living feels like death, and even the abyss of Emptiness seems by comparison a friendly place. Moreover, you have no choice, you cannot refuse the search, you cannot turn away from Truth.

Oddly, I have found that the end of the path includes the embrace of all that was there in the beginning. All of the anger exploding around me—and even should it explode within me—is taken into this capacious Emptiness where it is somehow welcomed and transmuted into love. How or why this happens, I can't say. But every once in a while a friend like Jacob comes along to prove it to me, violence matted in his hair, a smile on his radiant face. It's as if God were saying, "See, I told you. This is the Way. This is how it works. This is the path from Here to Here."

STILL IN THE BALL GAME

Much is said these days in books and on television specials about fulfilling wishes and learning how to intend what you want in your life, whether it be peace or happiness or simply money to pay the bills. The premise is that you are God, that you are the source of everything that appears in your world, and that therefore the world will reflect how you think and feel and act. Put out negative vibes, the world will dish up problems to match. Affirm what you want and act as though you already have it, presto!, it will appear.

And in the great drama of life, so it may. There is little doubt that the relative world tends to mirror what you believe, and that eventually you'll get what you give. However, while most of these quasi-philosophies assert the non-dual message that "God is everything and everything is God," they continue to teach that one can reach a state or obtain a thing that is somehow missing, which only reinforces the illusory notion of separation: the idea that there is a separate "you" who can get something that is "other than you." And it is this very message of "How to use your divinity to secure peace or fame or fortune" that denies the truth of your divinity! It leaves you, as a friend likes to say, "still in the ball game," still a separate "you" seeking a better situation somewhere or somewhen else, when all the while the Kingdom of Heaven is this very moment.

"Then why do anything?" you ask, the answer to which is "Try doing nothing!" That Which You Are—God Himself—is all the doing in the world, and carry on, by all means! In fact, the answer to the question "Why do anything?" is that you *are* anything! Intenders provide something you can do about your situation (a popular idea indeed!), assuming you are not entirely comfortable with it, rather than point out the fact that Who You Really Are can never be improved, for you are Perfection Itself, unchanging, appearing as any state, any thing.

For instance, when I see that I am not in prison but that prison is in Me, is, in other words, in this Pure Awareness that I am, I transcend all concepts of myself. What, therefore, is the reason to affirm yet another concept such as "I am peaceful, prosperous, or whatever"? Why pin myself down to yet another concept, considering that all such concepts are of "things"—phenomena—and are therefore indicative of the separate self? Somewhere along the path to Self-realization I came to see that God had been tapping me on the shoulder for a long time in an effort to wake me up. But was He tapping me so that I'd become Him—that which I already am—or so that I'd become a more peaceful and prosperous individual that was still separate from Him? (As if that were possible!)

The awakened ones say that a good teacher is one who leaves you with nothing. Truly no-thing at all. What is the point of saying "You are God" if one then tells you that because of that, you can be anyone or get anything you want? The truth is, you can't *be* anyone, because you're no-one. And you can't *get* anything, because you're all things. And ironically, profoundly realizing this, one realizes the "peace that passeth all understanding." And likewise, realizing that everything is oneself, one gains the "treasures in Heaven." "Seek ye first the Kingdom of Heaven," Christ said, "and all these things shall be added unto thee." Or as Douglas Harding so often and so aptly said, "See and see what happens."

Why settle for less?

BEFORE AWAKENING: ROACHES, BEDBUGS, AND SCABIES AFTER AWAKENING: ROACHES, BEDBUGS, AND SCABIES

I'm sorry, God, but some things in this world are just plain nasty.

For awhile in New York I lived on the Lower East Side in a tenement apartment that was owned, operated, and totally overrun with cockroaches. They eventually evicted me, and not because I didn't pay the rent.

When I first arrived in Honolulu I took a room in a large house at the edge of a jungle in Manoa Valley. There were geckos on the walls and ceiling, a welcome sight because I knew they dined on what otherwise might dine on me, and although the room smelled musty and damp, it was neat and clean. The homeowners, a Christian minister and his wife, assigned to me as part of the rent a small area in their refrigerator, and several nights later when I went to retrieve a container of juice and flipped on the kitchen light, I was stunned by what confronted me: monster-size roaches, the biggest I'd ever seen, hundreds, maybe thousands of them, more than my New York apartment could have held, all scurrying this way and that, retreating helter-skelter from the light, swarming over the dishes on the counter, the pots and pans in the sink, falling from the edge of the table to the floor. Needless to say, I moved soon after to another room in another house.

Years later in a Mexican prison, the very first night my fall-partner and I were there, we awoke scratching, and my partner's eyes were swollen shut. In the morning I helped him to the infirmary where a smirking nurse confirmed that we had been bitten by bedbugs, and for a year thereafter it was my nightly ritual to seek them out and destroy them, until finally I got used to them and let them bite. They were everywhere. They bored holes in the wall plaster and the two-by-fours of our makeshift "house," they infested our bedding and clothing, they hid in our shoes. There were zillions of them in every part of the prison, and we humans were no match.

This American prison by comparison is antiseptically clean, but wherever there are hundreds of people living in close proximity there is the danger of contagion. MRSA, the flesh-eating bacteria, hit the prison a decade ago; especially vulnerable were those who were sharing infected tattoo needles and ink. Then last year we were assaulted with scabies, all over the facility. MRSA aside, the scabies critter has to be the nastiest of all the no-see-ums, burrowing under the skin and proliferating in festering communities, causing an itch no amount of scratching will relieve. For those infected, days of quarantine followed, clothes and bedding were specially laundered, showers and medicated salves were administered, cells were disinfected. And still to this day an occasional flare-up occurs, and the process begins anew. I've been lucky, so far, but every pimple, every minor rash or occasional itch brings scrutiny and no small amount of concern on my part. Lord, let this body, this temporary form, collapse with heart failure or strangle with pneumonia or even waste away with some

God-awful cancerous rot, but please don't let it be eaten alive by a bug I can't even see!

And having said that, I noticed this tiny sore in the crick of my arm, an itch I dare not scratch....

SAINTS AND SINNERS

A friend here, a born-again Christian, once called me a saint on the inside and a sinner on the outside.

At least he got the outside part right.

Unless, perhaps unknowingly, he was referring to us all, for we are all built to that design, the One Alone manifesting as the separate many, the Divine Self appearing as the ordinary "me."

And contrary to what many spiritual seekers believe, realizing the One doesn't necessarily "fix" the many. Not only may the world continue doling out its share of difficulties, but the ordinary "me" may continue in its habitually neurotic ways. The difference is that, beneath the ego's rancor and foolishness, there is the knowledge of Pure Being, Awareness aware of Itself, undergirding all. Here is Gangaji, from her book *The Diamond In Your Pocket*: "There are moments of unhappiness, anger, and distress, there are moods that pass through, yet all is occurring on a ground of joy."

Which about sums it up, and no doubt better than I could.

And it's my experience that, although the ego may not radically change, certainly everything is more lightly held. Problems that the world doles out become less problematic or cease to be problems at all, and rancor in all its ugly forms simply no longer appears. While anger and distress may come and go, they do so more quickly, and moods no longer last for more than an hour or two. There is also the knowledge that everything presented is a reminder to come home to Who I Really Am. This is particularly true of difficulties, which can no longer pass without serving as taps on the shoulder, pointers to the Peaceful Awake Space they happen in. Moreover, there is the knowledge that everything presented *is* Who I Am: Awake Space manifesting as this and that and the "ten thousand things." Including the ego, which when seen from the vantage point of Awake Space, is embraced with love, even gratitude, no matter how foolish it appears. Know thy*Self* equals love thy*self*.

Incidentally, that same born-again Christian friend, when he found out I was a Buddhist, asked me if I had purchased any weaving material from our hobby canteen list.

"Weaving material?" I asked.

"Yeah," he said, "because you'd better learn how to weave a hand basket, seeing as how you're going to hell in one!"

PROPERTY

When I was thirty I bought an eighty-acre spread on a mesa west of the Rockies for ten thousand dollars. There was an old log cabin on it and several outbuildings, including an outhouse. The only running water in the cabin was pumped from a cistern to the kitchen sink, until a friend installed the plumbing for a hot-water heater and an old bathtub I found in a junkyard. Cold wasn't the word for that place in the winter. What warmth there was came from an ancient pot-belly stove in the kitchen, but little heat made it to the other rooms.

There were chickens: six hens and an ill-tempered Polish rooster. There were more than a dozen dogs and cats rescued from the nearest pound, all mutts. In the winter they slept together on the rickety porch in a ball of fur, and in the summer they roamed the mesa like wild animals.

After my daughter was born and when the weather turned mild in the spring, friends arrived, hippies from the cities to the east. They smoked dope and dropped acid and worked naked in the garden. All were young except for Cranky Frank, a white-bearded ex-con in his sixties with Kansas City mob connections. He charmed the locals in a nearby town, but he was a con man through and through and a good front-man for everything we needed where we couldn't go—even the town laundromat had a sign that read: "No Hippies!" That summer he bought a truck and an Airstream trailer and outfitted the trailer with secret compartments under the carpeted floor, stem to stern, and off he went to Mexico for a load of pot. He died two years later in an emergency room of a Kansas City hospital with a bag of weed in his pocket and a broken hip from a car accident. Friends said he gave up, just like that.

Then I bought a section out in New Mexico on the San Augustin Plain, up against BLM land. The house was adobe, and in a flat area behind the barn, a pal named Willy scraped out an airstrip amongst the sage and piñon, then dug an enormous hole at one end in which to hide plane loads of dope from Mexico. When the former owner showed up by surprise one day and found Willy digging the hole, Willy told him he was building a bomb shelter or a latrine, he wasn't sure which. That first plane trip on a moonless night, Willy forgot to turn on the airstrip lights, and the pilot crashed a mile short. It was a miracle the pilot and co-pilot survived.

The thing I remember most about both of those places was the silence. I can't say I spent more than a half year at either one, but it was enough that the silence got to me. There were too many stars in the night sky. There was no television, no place to go for a beer or a film. There was no excitement, no intrigue. There was too damn much peace.

A man who was here years ago used to talk about living off the grid when he got out, and then when he was released and finished parole he did just that—actually built his own house in the middle of nowhere in the high desert of New Mexico. To me it sounded like his dream come true, everything he ever wanted. Today he lives in Beverly Hills and sends me photos of him and his wife posing with celebrities. You never know. Maybe there was too damn much peace for him also.

Here, of course, there are no stars, and a moment of peace is a rare event. It is never silent, and the drama surely rivals that of a Hollywood studio. There are plenty of Cranky Franks here too, and a fair share of head-scratchers like Willy; even a few wrinkled hippies left over from the sixties. But what is gone is my quest for excitement and intrigue, and the belief that peace could ever be "outside" of Who I Am. Of course, I would love to gaze at the night sky and have the stars invade me, and I can't imagine the joy of being lost (or is it "found"?) in a forest of old growth trees (a recent parolee wrote to say that the first thing he did when he got out was drive to a park and hug a tree!).

Still, there are flowers here in certain areas, and grass, and hardy weeds near the fence outside my window, the occasional rabbit or squirrel, and the birds. And all manner of detritus trapped in the spider webs on the window panes and the bars beyond. These spiders—there must he twenty or more—how they wait, camouflaged in their shadowy dens, then race out to entomb a struggling fly in their silk! Talk about intrigue!

When I think back to those two ranches I bought, I realize above all that I never owned them, not in name, not in mind, and certainly not ultimately as a fact. I provided the money, but asked others to sign the deeds, and not for a minute did I feel at home in either place. There was, I suppose, a good lesson in being on the run and using false IDs all those years: As it turned out, accumulating possessions and leaving a trail of personal history was the last thing I needed.

But what have I ever owned? What has any of us truly possessed in our lives? As who we think we are—separate selves—we are "things" up against other things, be they ranches or cars or clothes. We are *next* to them. We may gather them close and even wear them, but like a coin in the hand, they could as easily own us as we own them.

Then again, what *haven't* I owned, and what haven't we (and not as "we") truly possessed? As Who I Really Am—this empty and aware Space for whatever fills it—I am the sole owner of all that is, the sole possessor of the "ten thousand things," and anyone can say the same. Everything is inside of this Awareness that I am, and I cannot own it more intimately than that. When this identity shift occurs, it occurs not by thinking about it but by looking-to-see, actually experiencing in the heart of the One Experiencer that everything is within, that, in fact, my true body is "All That Is."

Sometimes I look at my current so-called "possessions" and I have to laugh. Each inmate is issued a "Property Form" upon which is listed everything he owns, all of which, with the exception of the few appliances he is allowed to buy from the canteen, must fit into a standard size duffel bag. It is, by today's standards in the West, little more than the "shirt on your back." And to consider those few items my possessions and yet not the cell, the cellhouse itself and the yard outside and distant mountains, is surely absurd.

But what is even more amusing is the Property Form. It isn't big enough. To list all that I own as Who I Really Am would require the entire record of science and history itself, and so much more. Or perhaps there should be only one item on the list: "Universe."

This, then, is my home, and I see a good reason to care for it all. How I ever could have called this tiny fragment "me" and the rest "not me," I don't know. But then, obviously it was never up to "me" to begin with.

FORSAKEN

Illness doesn't often visit, but when it does, it makes up for lost time by yanking me out of whatever esoteric idea I have about Who I Really Am and slamming me head first into this sneezing, aching body I suddenly wish belonged to someone else. I once went eight years without a cold or the flu, not bad for an inmate living in a crowd, but lately I've been host to a nasty virus on a yearly basis, and every time it arrives I feel mentally and physically dense, trapped in an identity that won't do what it's told, like maybe feel better.

Ten years ago I underwent my first hip replacement surgery, and two years ago, the second. The first one went well, but the second one knocked me for a loop. When I came to, I felt giddy with relief that it was over, but by the end of the day I was vomiting what little I had eaten, and the nausea would continue throughout the night and for the better part of a week. The morphine drip, and later, every painkiller they tried, made me sick. I couldn't eat. Worse, I couldn't sleep. They took me off narcotics on the third day and brought me two over-the-counter Tylenol every six hours, and still the nausea continued. On the fourth day, because I couldn't bring myself to take a shower, I began to stink, and on the fifth day when they transported me from the hospital to the prison infirmary, I was delirious. And the crazy thing was, I was still seeing this wide-open Clarity here, even though I had completely contracted into the body. I *saw* this Space, and *felt* like a slug.

The night of the sixth day, I thought I was dying, and I distinctly heard a voice say, "God, why hast Thou forsaken me?", and shortly thereafter, I had an out-of-body experience in which I "floated" around the room, then passed through the wall and into the hallway beyond. It was dark, and although there was the lightness of being disembodied, there was also something ominous, as if I were about to descend into hell. And then when I returned to my body, I slept, and woke up in the morning without the nausea.

A year and a half later I related this story to a Seeing friend in the visiting room. As part of a prescribed therapy, she had recently endured a two-week, water-only fast during which she'd felt her body dying. When I told her about my illness in the hospital and the words I so clearly heard, she said, "So did I!" She too had completely contracted into her body at a time when it was under severe stress. And when I wrote to Richard Lang in London about this, he said, "Yes, that's the way of it," implying that conscious attention is placed exactly where and when it is needed, and that what you think you want isn't always the answer. The ultimate answer, of course, lies in the fact that who you are is not exclusively the body, which is to say that the answer to the question, "Why hast Thou forsaken me?" is that He hasn't! Each time we appear to contract, whether we are under duress or not, we descend into hell, and when we return to the realization of Who We Really Are—this One Conscious Capacity and all that it is capacity for—we are resurrected. And in that glorious return, we are all resurrected as the Eternal Christ, First Person Singular, The Alone.

In this particular cellhouse the cells are "dry;" that is, there are no facilities in the cells, and one must use a common area where there are sinks and toilets in a sort of bathroom-down-the-hall for 50. Since moving here from a "wet" cell in another cellhouse, I've become a bit of a germaphobe, washing my hands perhaps more than needed. But after my experience in the hospital, there has been a noticeable space between this Conscious Capacity and these hands washing themselves, between Who I Really Am and these cumbersome thoughts about what a drag it is to be sick in prison. Out of any given year, rarely does a month go by when there isn't at least one inmate hacking and wheezing, and that too seems to be the way of it, life doing its thing, whether or not I agree.

In July I caught a whopper of a summer cold, and despite the heavy thoughts and the hands that kept on washing themselves—after all, there are 49 others *without* a cold—I was okay with it; in fact, much more than okay: I was grateful for the opportunity to so clearly see the difference between Who I Really Am here, and what I appear as there; this Awake Cold-free Emptiness here, and that aching, shivering body there.

Not to mention the oh-so-odd-and-amusing sensation of all that wheezing, sneezing, coughing and snorting going on in this luminous space where I once thought I had a head!

TIME AND TIME AGAIN

Recently I read an author who was expounding on how many seconds he'd been alive and how he was not the same person at two or twenty-five or fifty that he was today, which in his view was a way to disengage from the belief that he was a solid, self-existing entity called a bodymind.

But isn't it easier and more convincing to simply *look* at this empty and aware capacity you are looking out of and *see* that you've never been alive for the briefest of moments, that in fact you are timeless, that time and all of creation pass *through* you? Pure Awareness—that which you are—is no-thing, and where there is no-thing there is no movement and therefore no measure of time.

When I was sentenced for this case, I thought, "How in the world am I going to do all this time?" Now, thirty years have passed in what seems like the blink of an eye, and isn't that exactly what it is—a mere blink, and it is gone; one blink, and it was never there? Byron Katie once said, "Everything you think happened didn't." There is always only this simple presence, this aware empty capacity for thoughts and memories and the scene appearing now and never then. The stories we tell are the sum total of our "existence," and I find them endlessly fascinating, even though, in a sense, they are the same story told over and over.

There is perhaps another way to look at the

phenomenon of time, a way that seems to be a more recent conclusion of some cosmologists, one that is at least mathematically possible—that all of time, from the Big Bang on and into an endless future (or until the Big Crunch when the universe is drawn back in to a point of singularity), exists simultaneously in a kind of multi-dimensional tube containing all that ever happened and all that ever will happen. It's akin to the analogy of the fly walking across a painting: the part of the painting it has already crossed it considers the "past," and the part it hasn't yet come to it considers the "future," but when it takes off and looks back it sees the whole painting all at once, the entire past and future presented statically in the now-moment. It was the fly's *interpretation* that loaned a past and a future to the painting, just as it is our interpretation that we live a "life" travelling from a past into a future.

If the fly could have laughed, certainly it would have, and why shouldn't we, considering our folly? Moreover, it's as if we think we can change the course of history, that we can willfully make a difference, when in fact we are all the differences that ever were or could be. Said another way, it's as if we think that each of us as separate individuals are responsible for our past and future, when what we really are is altogether outside the concept of time, is the timeless awake emptiness in which all of time appears, moment by moment or all at once, which, when it comes down to it, are one and the same. Isn't the profound understanding of that the end of our story and the beginning of the simple presence of what we really are? And won't one look in the right direction confirm it?

WORLD-AS-MIRROR

Almost all of the great upheavals or course changes in my life have occurred during the vernal or autumnal equinoxes. Even the minor changes seem to be more frequent or more noticeable during these times.

And now it's September and the world has been snapping at me all week: An inmate scolded me in his work area for leaving a mess I didn't leave; an officer accused me of lying, and in reviewing what I'd said from his point of view, I realized he was right; the prison went on lockdown and I missed a long-awaited barber appointment; the canteen quit selling typewriter ribbons for my brand of typewriter; and all week long no mail has arrived, at least not for me.

There are a couple of old neurotic reactions in my kit bag to these minor calamities. One is to push back, and in so doing make things worse. The other is to give up, and declare myself a victim of whatever injustice—real or imagined—I've suffered at the hands of another person, the state, or God Himself. Of course, in the past, a few of the upheavals were boons, arriving unexpectedly and with no small measure of appreciation, but most were the negative variety, sudden downturns that left me angry or frustrated or at the very least feeling sorry for myself. Not one did I consider a "challenge."

But, as they say, it's a whole new ball game now. For instance, I know without doubt that the world, each scene that appears, is a mirror of the thoughts happening here, or more accurately, of the attachment to the thoughts. I am thus directed back to myself as the one who is responsible for all that appears, and moreover, directed to inquire about those thoughts and see who they belong to. Ultimately, then, the world mirrored back exposes the thoughts at the root of all thought: the belief in an intrinsically real and separate self living in a world of separate things that must somehow be manipulated to one's advantage. In other words, the world-as-mirror returns me to Reality, to Who I Really Am, to what was there all along but simply wasn't noticed.

And that which is noticed is one's emptiness, one's primordial awakeness, the awareness right "here" that embraces all that appears "there." The world-as-mirror, then, is seen to be not the final realization, but a pointer back to the truth, a step in the right direction, and that direction is *this* way, always and ever Here. There is no something "there" being mirrored back to another something "here." There is only THIS RIGHT HERE, aware no-thing manifesting as anything. In other words, that which is mirrored back to you is you, be it a chair, a building, a boon or a calamity. And that which appears is all that you can be said to be, moment by moment, for "you" have disappeared and been replaced by the scene. That which you once thought was "you" here seeing "mountains and rivers" there, subject viewing objects, is now seen to be simply "mountains and rivers," pure non-dual subjectivity, Who You Really Are.

Some would call this "surrender," and in a sense perhaps it is, although it is not something done by a separate "you," nor is there anything separate to be surrendered to something else. And yet I find this surrender to occur, and not once and for all but repeatedly, time (and time again) surrendered into Timelessness, "self" and "other" returning to Self from whom they never left. This, it would seem, is the mechanism by which the universe appears, the great game of life and death in all its joy and terror and without which there would be nothing at all.

So I applaud the game, and am deeply grateful, especially at this time of year when I am so clearly reminded to come Home, come Home.

ALL IS ONE AND ONE IS ALL

It's hunting season, and today I watched ten deer feed along the side of the perimeter road, then amble nonchalantly into the staff parking lot. How is it they know when to exchange places with those who would hunt them? Do they silently laugh while we humans schlep our cannons into the high country in search of prey that is no longer there?

And what about birds or butterflies that migrate thousands of miles to the same area each year? Do they really navigate using landmarks or magnetic forces, as we surmise, or do they just go? These mysteries of nature that we insist are not mysteries, can we solve them with our stories, our so-called "facts"?

Each year when the swallows depart, part of me departs with them. All summer they are here, diving and banking and scouring the air a foot above the ground, and then a day or two before the first freeze they are gone, leaving empty nests beneath the eaves. How do they know when to leave, and where do they go for the winter; where do they stop along the way?

I said to a friend one day in the recreation yard after a swallow whizzed by, "How would you like to fly like that, pure stillness in the wind, the earth rocketing by beneath you?" He blinked, and said, "Yeah," and then he blinked again, and I could hear the wheels turning in his head, the questions about my having it backwards.

A minute later he said, "Not sure I could eat the bugs, though."

Bugs. Bugs, and more bugs. Each peering from the same single Eye we all do. A man two cells down woke up one morning to a long line of tiny black ants emerging from a crack at the base of the cement wall and proceeding single file to the other side of the room and up the side of his locker box, then under the metal lid and down into the box where they had bored a tiny hole in a plastic bag filled with holiday chocolates, for convict and bug a treasure if ever there was one, at least around here. He plugged the crack, he threw away the chocolates, he killed the ants. I thought he should have placed the bag in front of the crack.

My favorite bug is the dragonfly. I watched one hover, then flit, then hover, then flit—right in front of me as I strolled the track around the softball field. It seemed to be performing its dance just for me, at times so close I could almost touch it.

My second favorite bug is the praying mantis. It used to be my favorite, but I found one stranded in the cellhouse one day, and when I went to pick it up, it bit me. I used to like ladybugs too, but last year we experienced what the local news called an "infestation" of them, and these were the kind of ladybugs that, when they landed on you, bit like a horsefly. I thought ladybugs ate aphids.

I heard a scientist say on the radio that ravens are the smartest birds. They problem solve. They have their own language of movements and calls. Turkeys, I've heard, are the dumbest, which I suppose is why some people call other people "turkey." But last year I saw a nature show on PBS about how surprisingly intelligent wild turkeys are, how subtle and complex are their communication skills, how they display individual personalities and even emotions. Of course, I don't know about the turkeys raised in crowded cages until they are big enough and fat enough to lose their heads and be fed to humans. They may be stupid, having been bred that way.

I sometimes imagine that the public, if they think of prisoners at all, think of us as these sort of industrial turkeys, caged and fed and living in our stink. In a sense, we are. But we're not stupid. We may be dumbed down a little because we're out of the game and on the bench, but we still have our signs and calls and displays of emotion. Sometimes we even solve problems. And although the public may call for our heads, the vast majority of us will get to keep them, although I'm not sure that means we'll be any smarter.

But here is the point I wanted to make when I started this chapter: How do deer and birds and insects know what to do and where to go? Is it not because they are the movement of the ALL, just as we humans are, just as everything is? Simply that? For every last one of us is the One, expressing Itself. Even us turkeys here in our cages. Even when we did what we did to get here.

DEPARTURES

One thing about prison is that you get to know many people—you live and work with them for years, even decades—and then when they are paroled or are transferred to another prison, you never see them again. In the last 30 years I can't count the number of friends who have departed. They move on with their lives. They forget or at least want to forget about where they've been, and even what they did to get there.

Recently a friend was told that his parole was approved and that he is leaving next week. When he came to my cell he said he was both worried and over-joyed, and I noticed that he had already bitten his finger-nails to the quick. I shook his hand, and he told me he wished I were leaving with him, wished that I too could walk out of this hellhole and into the free world. And when I thanked him and said that it didn't happen that way, I knew he thought I meant the obvious, but what I really meant was that no one for themselves has ever left Who They Really Are, and that for me it is impossible to see this place as a hellhole, not when it is seen within this divine Emptiness, this same Emptiness that is free-dom itself.

When I was a boy, my grandfather and both my grandmothers died. These were departures I wasn't pre-pared for. Suddenly those who had seemed so permanent were no longer there. Aunts and uncles disappeared in the same manner, and then my mother died and I remember thinking that there was no going back, no one to rely one.

It was different when my son died. I never relied on him, and in many ways I never knew him, but when I first heard he was gone it was as though I had lost a part of myself, an extension of who I thought I was. Now, thankfully, that mistaken view is gone, along with the mistaken view I once held about him, and I see and know him for Who He Really Is, right here in this One Emptiness that we are.

There is a valuable lesson in all of these departures, these continuous exits, and that lesson is that, while everything passes, I don't. When I look back and see this Aware Emptiness, I know that everything that ever appeared in my life—every person, every scene, every split second—also disappeared, moment by moment. There was, and is, nothing to hold onto, not one person or thing. Moreover, the same applies to this body and mind. Although it appears more often than other phenomena, it is clearly no more than a succession of scenes strung together like frames of a film, each one instantly departing like all the rest. But the one thing that never departs is this Aware No-thing, this visibly obvious Emptiness within which the scenes appear. With nothing to hold onto, this No-thing has to be me, has to be what I really am.

And so it is obvious that I have never gone anywhere. Everything arrives and departs within me, entirely on its own, while I never leave, never move by so much as an inch. And thank God!—Can you imagine a world in which a thing or an event or an emotion arrives and never leaves? Surely that would be hell—as hellish as the belief in an intrinsically existing "self" that lasts through time. But as to this Emptiness, where could No-thing go? Where could God go that isn't already Him- or Herself?

And of course, of all the departures in my life, the departure of this "self," this ego, was the most welcome. Not that it disappeared altogether, but it no longer occupied the central position, was no longer seen to be who I am. Rather, it was, and still is, one of the appearances that come and go in this central No-thing, one of a myriad of manifestations that this Aware Emptiness is empty for. Who I Really Am functions through it, and seen in this way it is seen with love, it is forgiven, it is God manifesting as this body and mind.

Speaking of this body-mind, it is not only out of the central position, off its imagined throne, as it were, but it seems intent on getting out of the picture altogether. There is strong evidence that it is departing, albeit piecemeal, folding and flaking toward oblivion, and if these thoughts constitute what others call my mind, it's a mind less crowded day by day. What becomes of it in the meantime is anyone's guess, but eventually the body at least may be headed for "Boot Hill," the prison cemetery on a mesa across the river. The going joke is that to conserve room they bury convicts standing up, and God help you if they drop you in upside-down, head over heels for eternity! Especially if you think you have a head.

Then there is this book. Each word, sentence, paragraph and chapter has arrived and departed within the awake expanse of this Emptiness, and no doubt sooner than later the entire book will depart as well, like everything else. All will be gone except for this timeless and spaceless Emptiness within which all of time and space appear.

And what never fails to astonish, no matter how many times I repeat it, is the knowledge that everything that passes through this Emptiness *is* this Emptiness, manifesting Itself endless times in endless ways, always right here and always right now. In the deepest sense, nothing ever departs, for nothing ever arrived. It was all along Pure Subjectivity, is and ever shall be. Pure Subjectivity observing Itself, loving Itself, astonishing Itself.

We cannot depart, no matter how hard we try. This is it. Just THIS!

ACKNOWLEDGMENTS

My sincere thanks to Jan for helping with this book. Also to Julian Noyce at Non-Duality Press, Richard Lang, Catherine Harding, Joe Ayers, Fr. Bob, and so many others. Love and appreciation to all.

For more information on the Headless Way of Douglas Harding and the awareness experiments that allow you to see for yourself Who You Really Are, visit:

www.headless.org

ABOUT THE AUTHOR

J.C. Amberchele was born in Philadelphia in 1940. In the 1980's after he went to prison, he began meditating and studying the works of Wei Wu Wei and others, until he happened upon an article by Douglas Harding and actually *saw* Who he really is. Since then, he has been practicing Seeing, and is the author of three previous books on the subject, all published by Non-Duality Press. He has been incarcerated for more than 30 years.

Conscious.tv is a TV channel which broadcasts on the internet at www.conscious.tv. It also has programmes shown on several satellite and cable channels around the world including the Sky system in the UK where you can watch programmes at 8.30 pm every evening on channel No. 192. The channel aims to stimulate debate, question, enquire, inform, enlighten, encourage and inspire people in the areas of Consciousness, Non-Duality and Science. It also has a section called 'Life Stories' with many fascinating interviews.

There are over 200 interviews to watch including several with communicators on Non-Duality including Richard Bates, Burgs, Billy Doyle, Bob Fergeson, Jeff Foster, Steve Ford, Suzanne Foxton, Gangaji, Greg Goode, Scott Kiloby, Richard Lang, Francis Lucille, Roger Linden, Wayne Liquorman, Jac O'Keefe, Mooji, Catherine Noyce, Tony Parsons, Halina Pytlasinska, Genpo Roshi, Satyananda, Richard Sylvester, Rupert Spira, Florian Schlosser, Mandi Solk, James Swartz, Art Ticknor, Joan Tollifson, and Pamela Wilson. There is also an interview with UG Krishnamurti. Some of these interviewees also have books available from Non-Duality Press.

Do check out the channel as we are interested in your feedback and any ideas you may have for future programmes. Email us at info@conscious.tv with your ideas or if you would like to be on our email newsletter list.

WWW.CONSCIOUS.TV

Books *from*
Non-Duality Press

If you enjoyed this book you might be interested in other titles published by Non-Duality Press.

Lightning Source UK Ltd.
Milton Keynes UK
UKOW05f0603270714

235819UK00001B/3/P